A Special Note
from Stormie Omartian

Bestselling Author of The Power of a Praying Wife

THE BOONE FAMILY has been an important and influential part of my life for over forty years and I love them all more than they will ever know. The power of their faith and their understanding of the right way to live in order to keep a family strong is more than impressive. It is a force that cannot be denied. And I have seen it lived out in each of them over decades.

When I got the call to pray for Ryan after his terrible accident, I knew the gravity of the situation and that a miracle was needed for him to even live through the night. As it turns out, that was only the beginning of countless miracles that were necessary for him to survive. He was so badly injured that there is no explanation as to why he not only survived but has come as far as he has today—and is still progressing—other than the miraculous power of God. I have not stopped praying for him, nor will I ever.

Lindy's book is more than a miraculous account of the long and painful life-and-death struggle her son, Ryan, has gone through. It is also the story of a courageous family and the mother of a severely injured child whose love was so strong that she refused to give up on the miracles she believed were possible—even in the face of everything telling her otherwise. This is a book about undying love, raw despair, unwavering hope, and faith so strong that it refuses to weaken. It is a gut-wrenchingly honest human portrait of facing what every parent or grandparent fears. It is about the struggle of trying to give beyond what is humanly possible and then finding strength outside of oneself to do so. This situation changed the lives of all who were involved in it, and it will change your life as well as you read it. It did that for me, and my life is the better for it.

When I started reading *Heaven Hears*, I simply couldn't put the book down until I finished it. Ryan's story touched me deeply, and I know it will touch your heart as well.

Praise for *Heaven Hears*

"This is a wonderful book. I am proud to have played a small part in this incredible story of love and recovery. It is a must for your library."

LARRY KING

"This is one of the most amazing stories of love I've ever witnessed."

RICK WARREN
Pastor of Saddleback Church and author of *The Purpose Driven Life*

"*Heaven Hears* is a powerful, inspirational story that all should read."

DR. DANIEL AMEN
Physician, bestselling author, and co-architect of The Daniel Plan

"I have known Pat and Shirley Boone for forty years, and I know that they know how to pray. When Ryan had the accident, Lindy and her family knew how to stand on the Word of God. As they prayed and believed God and didn't give up, miracles began to take place. When Jesus begins a good work, he will complete it. *Heaven Hears* will help you to know that nothing is too hard for God, and that you will win the battle, if you don't give up too soon. I salute this family."

DODIE OSTEEN
Cofounder of Lakewood Church, Houston, Texas

"I have known Lindy Boone Michaelis since she was a young girl. She has the heart of a never-quit, never-give-up spiritual warrior that most people don't have. Anyone can have it, but most don't. The seed of victory was first planted in her by her parents, Pat and Shirley Boone, but the staying power that it takes to never accept defeat comes only from the Word of God and total commitment to stand on it, no matter what. That's Lindy! She is a heroine of faith, not only for Ryan, but for her entire family. *Heaven Hears* is the story of that faith. You can have that kind of faith, but you'll have to do what Lindy has done to get it. Read about it. Pray for her as you live it with her. It's an ongoing miracle that already has a marvelous outcome, but it's not over yet. The best is yet to come. Here is the *key*—Jesus is Lord!"

KENNETH COPELAND
Founder of Kenneth Copeland Ministries

"By every measure I know God's Word to reveal, *Heaven Hears* stands as a beautiful, truthful, grace-filled testimony to the power of simple-yet-unrelenting prayer and faith in God's love and his healing promises. The sheer fact of Ryan Corbin's being alive today (not to mention his amazing and continual progress), joined to the unshakable constancy of his mother's and her family's ironclad refusal to surrender 'believing,' give us a clear-cut testimony to a completely believable 'miracle-in-motion.' Lindy Michaelis's story will stimulate practical, faith-in-action hope for any person in any situation.

"As a pastor-friend who has observed this epic from

the beginning, I urge readers: lift your eyes and open your heart to this truth—God's changeless love and his Son's unchanging grace are for us all today. *Heaven Hears* gives us Ryan Corbin's case study as a reminder and a call to embrace the eternal promise: 'All things are possible to those who believe!'"

PASTOR JACK W. HAYFORD
Chancellor of The King's University–Los Angeles and founding pastor of The Church On The Way

"Our son Steven was the person directly behind Ryan when he fell through the skylight, a day which changed all of our lives. We have witnessed this tragic near-fatal accident, this miracle of recovery, and this family that refused to believe anything but the best possible recovery. If ever a mother and family willed and prayed someone to stay with them for a higher calling, it was Lindy, her family, and the Boone family. They did this for Ryan. As someone has said, 'Prayer is the greatest wireless connection.' The Boone family had this connection and have kept it blazing for years! A true account of the power of prayer and the power of faith, hope, and love!"

BILL AND TANI AUSTIN
The Starkey Foundation

"Lindy Boone Michaelis, in her beautiful book *Heaven Hears*, reminds us that prayer is powerful. God knows us and the tiniest details of our lives, and even when it's hard to understand why we are in a difficult situation, we know that he is able to take our brokenness and reconstruct something with beauty and purpose. Heaven hears all of our cries and sighs, our pleas and petitions, and our praises and rejoicing. I believe this book will touch your heart."

ROMA DOWNEY
Actress on the television series *Touched by an Angel*

HEAVEN HEARS

THE TRUE STORY OF WHAT HAPPENED
WHEN PAT BOONE ASKED THE WORLD TO PRAY
FOR HIS GRANDSON'S SURVIVAL

HEAVEN HEARS

LINDY BOONE MICHAELIS
with Susy Flory

Tyndale House Publishers, Inc.
Carol Stream, Illinois

Visit Tyndale online at www.tyndale.com.

TYNDALE and Tyndale's quill logo are registered trademarks of Tyndale House Publishers, Inc.

Heaven Hears: The True Story of What Happened When Pat Boone Asked the World to Pray for His Grandson's Survival

Designed by Ron Kaufmann

Published in association with MacGregor Literary, Inc., of Hillsboro, OR.

ISBN 978-1-4143-8324-8

Printed in the United States of America

19	18	17	16	15	14	13
7	6	5	4	3	2	1

To all those who have received that terrible phone call about a loved one—injured, in the hospital, or in a crisis—and filled the waiting rooms, in pain and in prayer. I wrote this book for you. May you discover the faithfulness of the Father as I have.

Contents

Foreword

BY PAT BOONE

Blessed be the God and Father of our Lord Jesus Christ,
the Father of mercies and God of all comfort, who comforts
us in all our affliction, so that we may be able to comfort
those who are in any affliction, with the comfort with
which we ourselves are comforted by God.

2 CORINTHIANS 1:3-4, ESV

THOSE VERSES from God's Word sound so empathetic and helpful and . . . well, *comforting*, don't they? And they are. But the requirement for receiving God's comfort is being *afflicted*. And we, as a family, surely have been. Especially Ryan, Lindy's son and my beloved grandson.

Big, handsome, intelligent, and good-hearted, Ryan was hurt so grievously that the doctors at UCLA doubted he would live through the first night. Until then, our large and growing family had been so blessed that it seemed we might make it through this life with only minor scars. But from the moment Ryan fell almost forty feet through the skylight of an apartment building in West Los Angeles, our lives were all affected—and afflicted.

How could this have happened to our first grandchild; the first boy; the happy, outgoing, talented young man with such a promising future, engaged to be married in just a few months? How could our loving God have *allowed* this to happen? How could our separate and combined lives go on as before? If Ryan lived, would he ever be the same? Would we?

When we realized how seriously he had been injured, our hearts stopped. All our plans for the immediate future came to a halt. Even long-term plans were now in question. We could scarcely think of anything but Ryan, what he was going through, and whether we could pray him back to some kind of health and normalcy. During the first days and weeks, we were all just praying for Ryan to be able to breathe on his own.

That's affliction.

And where could we turn for any comfort, any hope, any promise?

Friend, you know there's only one place—and that's where we all turned. We huddled and prayed together in the hospital waiting room, in the halls, and out on the grounds. We called every church and Christian TV prayer line we could think of. We called our minister friends across America, and they assured us they'd prompt their congregations and audiences to pray for Ryan. CNN's Larry King called to ask if I'd like to come on his highly popular TV show to ask millions around the world to pray for our grandson and for us. Dear Lindy, our daughter and Ryan's mom, and I accepted his invitation. An estimated fifty million people worldwide saw each program and were asked to join us in prayer.

God is where you turn in the midst of a crisis. God is the source of real comfort. Family and friends do what they can, but they can't give you divine assurance; they can't intervene and decree your loved one's healing; they can't actually cause it to happen. Only God can do those things. And so we prayed, fervently and continually.

In fact, on the day after the horrible accident—while Ryan was in a deep coma, on every kind of life support, with tubes and gadgets sticking out of his head—I laid my hand on his chest and prayed as I never had before: "Lord, you filled this boy with your Holy Spirit when he was only four years old. You've made this beautiful body and brain your dwelling place since then. I'm not asking you to reach down to touch and heal Ryan . . . *I'm asking you to rise up in him, and heal every cell and ruptured place in this temple of your Spirit . . . from within him!*"

And that's what our loving Lord has done, over these long twelve years. In answering our countless prayers, he has involved the prayers and support of so many people in many ways. His greatest human instrument by far has been Ryan's incredible mother . . . our daughter Lindy. This whole ordeal is Lindy's story, the account of her indomitable, constant hold on God's promises and power and grace. As members of our extended family have rallied in every way we could think of, Lindy has been the linchpin, the quarterback calling the plays. She has creatively tried and changed various therapies; found wonderfully capable caregivers to care for Ryan in twelve-hour shifts around the clock; and worked tirelessly with her son to encourage his own commitment, faith, and patience in his interminable saga of recovery. All the while Lindy has continued to be a wonderful wife and mother to her other kids.

Along with her own mom, Shirley, Lindy has consistently read God's Word to Ryan and helped him memorize and repeatedly quote the promises of his heavenly Father.

Though you're about to read her account of this triumphant journey, even she can't fully convey how long it has seemed, how many times it appeared hopeless, how many times we, her family, have cried out to God, "Why, Lord, *why? Why is it taking so long?* You could just speak the word, and Ryan would be whole, restored, miraculously healed, to your own glory! *Why, Lord, why?*"

And that's the point of this foreword. Why, indeed?

I believe Ryan's miracle, the proof that heaven hears, has been allowed by God to stretch out over so long . . . because so many others go through even longer trials. They cry out the same plaintive questions, challenged to the limit as the years go by with seemingly declining prospects of change or healing. This story, Ryan and Lindy's story—ultimately God's story—was written to comfort those who are in any affliction, even those who have endured for years, "with the comfort with which we ourselves" have been comforted, encouraged, bolstered, and finally rewarded by God, in his infinite purpose and grace.

As long as it has been—and while he still has some ways to go—Lindy, Ryan, and the rest of us rejoice in how our faith has been tested, challenged, and deepened, and how it has grown. We are all the better for it, and though we would have avoided it if we'd had the choice, we see God's fingerprints on all that has happened. We pray he will use our experience to build the faith of others—and to comfort them in their affliction.

Introduction

"Do you believe, Lindy, in prayer?"

Larry King leaned forward in his chair, elbows on the table, his gaze sympathetic but searching.

"Oh, yes."

"Even though it has been two months."

"Oh, yes."[1]

I felt as if I were in the hot seat. It was my second appearance on *Larry King Live* in as many months, and I knew Larry was asking me the same question millions of viewers had: Does God really hear when we cry out to him?

"You've been praying for two months," Larry said.

"Yes."

Eight weeks before, life as I'd known it had been completely upended when my twenty-four-year-old son, Ryan, stepped through a skylight and fell three full stories. His skull was fractured, his lungs collapsed, and his heart stopped. When he broke through that roof, Ryan fell into a very different life, teetering on the edge of eternity.

For weeks my firstborn child lingered between life and death in the Intensive Care Unit at UCLA Medical Center. At first I was in shock, grieving, looking for answers. I felt so helpless; prayer was my lifeline.

Yet I wanted to do more. What I hadn't expected was

an opportunity to appear before a worldwide audience, all because Larry King was a friend of my dad, Pat Boone. Daddy had been friends with Larry since the talk-show icon had hosted a local radio show from a Miami hotel lounge back in the late 1950s. At the time, my dad was one of the most popular charting artists in the country (second only to Elvis Presley). Larry invited him to be a guest on his show, and they immediately hit it off. Over forty years later, Larry had made a name for himself as host of *Larry King Live*, CNN's most-watched and longest-running program.

Given their long-standing friendship, Daddy wasn't too surprised when he got a call from Larry's producer shortly after Ryan's accident. The producer said Larry had heard about Ryan's accident and wanted Daddy and me to come on the show for a few minutes so that people would hear about Ryan's accident and pray for him.

Even though Daddy wasn't surprised by the call, he thought the reason for the invitation was extraordinary. "He's giving us a platform," he told me.

I wasn't sure I could do it. "I feel too raw. I am a gaping wound. How do I talk about this in public? It's all too horrible."

But we decided to accept the invitation. Ryan needed every prayer he could get. Our first appearance on July 26, 2001, was short—a small segment at the end of one of Larry's programs. Daddy and I had been given just enough time to let viewers know about Ryan's accident and ask them to pray for his recovery.

The response to our first appearance was, as Larry said,

"almost unbelievable"; in fact, for days afterward UCLA Medical Center had been besieged with calls from people asking about Ryan.

Larry invited us back to his show three weeks later. Now my dad and I sat across from him for a second time. I didn't have to wait long before Larry followed up with another question.

"Why not? Why not an answer?"

"Can I read you something real quick?" I asked, reaching for the Bible I'd brought with me. Given the ups and downs of the past few weeks, I had few insights of my own.

"One thing the Lord has been trying to work in me," I said, as I flipped to the book of Romans, "is patience. And I rely more heavily on what he says in his Word now than ever before."

Finding the passage I'd been looking for, I began reading aloud: "We can rejoice, too, when we run into problems and trials, for we know that they are good for us—they help us learn to endure. And endurance develops strength of character in us, and character strengthens our confident expectation of salvation."[2]

I'm not sure this was the "answer" Larry or his audience was looking for, yet it was already clear to me that God was up to something. I was still working on what that passage meant, but I knew I had a big trial (that was an understatement), and I was told to rejoice because I would gain endurance, strength of character, and a confident expectation of salvation through it. My job was to hold fast to his Word and to do so in front of millions. I knew this was a rare opportunity to let viewers witness faith in action, even if it was the size of the proverbial mustard seed.

"I'm learning patience through this," I said. "But I still believe that my son is going to get better."

About forty-five minutes later, Larry gave the last word of the night to my dad, who once again asked people to pray.

And boy, did they pray. *Heaven Hears* is the story of what happened next. It's a story about the power of prayer. It's about miracles. It's about overcoming despair, persisting through suffering, and surviving against all odds.

It's an unbelievable story, and it's not over yet.

If you or someone you love has experienced a traumatic injury, you know that it's like a hallucinatory roller-coaster ride operated by a madman. There are tremendous ups and downs, not to mention sharp, jerky turns and dips that make your stomach tie up in knots. There are moments of triumph and joy and excitement, but there are also tears and screams and moments where you hold on until your knuckles turn white.

I'm still on that roller coaster, although it's slowed down a bit and the twists and turns aren't quite as bad these days. I've learned a few things along the way: that we are spiritual beings, here for a reason. That good things can come from bad. And that heaven does hear—even before we have a chance to look up.

CHAPTER I

THROUGH THE SKYLIGHT

We are not human beings having a spiritual experience.
We are spiritual beings having a human experience.

PIERRE TEILHARD DE CHARDIN

RYAN AND HIS ROOMMATES were always on a quest to look
good. After all, they were young guys living in LA and hoping
to make it in the entertainment business. Even though the
dangers of skin cancer were well known by 2001, a golden
tan was still status quo in Southern California. In that way,
I think Ryan took after me and his grandfather Pat.

The problem with his quest for the perfect tan was that
Ryan lived in an old stucco Brentwood apartment building
far from the beach. He did have access to a swimming pool
next door, but the apartment buildings on Dorothy Street
were built around central courtyards, almost like a picture
frame, and the sun's rays didn't last long before they passed
into shadow.

In the middle of Ryan's building was a garden with
concrete pathways. Framed around it were three stories
of apartments. The front door of each apartment opened
up to a walkway that ran around the inside of the frame.
Instead of a metal railing, each walkway was bordered by

1

a three-and-a-half-foot concrete wall on the courtyard side. Ryan and his roommates lived on the second floor in apartment 208. On the third floor was a stairway that led up to a roof-access door. The building was full of young professionals, so it wasn't uncommon for people to head up to the roof to sunbathe once the sun's rays moved on from the courtyard.

One sunny June day, Ryan got home from his job at California Pizza Kitchen at about three in the afternoon; his job on a television show was on hiatus so he worked as a server at the pizza restaurant to pay the bills. Ryan changed into shorts and flip-flops, threw on a black backpack holding his keys and a few other odds and ends, grabbed a towel, and invited his two roommates to come along. Grant was playing a video game and passed, but Steve decided he could use some sun too. The two of them headed upstairs, laughing and joking about their latest get-fit-and-good-looking schemes. They climbed the stairs to the roof-access door. It was closed but unlocked. Ryan went first.

After he stepped out into the bright afternoon sun, Ryan skirted to the left around a metal railing and then turned right to walk alongside it. To his left was a skylight flush with the roof. The skylight was designed to let in fresh air and natural light to the darker nooks and crannies of the apartment walkways. But at some point, probably due to the heat of the sun or maybe even rainwater problems, the four-by-eight-foot opening had been covered with a corrugated fiberglass panel, tacked down around the edges. Over the years and with exposure to the elements, the fiberglass cover had grown brittle and faded to almost perfectly match the color, and even the texture, of the rocks and pebbles on the tar-and-gravel roof.

Ryan walked along the pathway between the metal railing on his right and the skylight on his left. The path was no more than two feet wide; Steve followed about four feet behind. Ryan was almost past the skylight when Steve saw his roommate's left foot come down on the corner. Ryan's size 14 flip-flops bridged over the corner with his toes and heel still on the roof but the middle of his foot, bearing his weight, pressed down and the fiberglass started to flex inward. His right foot was still on the roof but as the fiberglass panel began to give way, his left foot started sliding toward the middle of the skylight. There was nothing beneath to bear his weight. As his foot slid inward, his body rotated around toward Steve, and Ryan looked straight into his roommate's eyes, surprised, and fell down through the fiberglass panel. There wasn't much noise except for the cracking of the fiberglass and a few thumps. Ryan was gone.

✦ ✦ ✦

I was dreaming of sunshine and beaches when the phone started ringing.

Where am I?

It was dark, and I was disoriented. Finally I remembered. I was on vacation with my husband, Mike, and our thirteen-year-old son, Tyler, in Málaga, Spain. We'd been at a time-share condo for about four or five days. During the day, I worked out and enjoyed the pool while Mike and Tyler played golf. One day we'd driven our rental car to a picturesque village at the top of a narrow, winding road. On another, Tyler had tried out parasailing. We'd even talked about a day trip to Morocco.

But for now I was sound asleep after a full day of sun and seafood. *So where is that ringing coming from?* Mike was still asleep, so I got out of bed and bumped my way out of the bedroom toward the sound in the living room. Tyler was asleep on the sofa bed—I couldn't believe he slept through the noise.

I finally found the phone and picked it up. "Lindy, we've been trying to reach you."

It was my sister Debby. Between the late-night call and the tone of her voice, I knew I'd better brace myself. It had to be bad.

"Nobody knew the number where you were staying. It's Ryan. He's had an accident." My breath caught in my throat.

"Not a car accident. He fell when he was on the roof of his apartment building. He and Steve were going up to get some sun but Ryan somehow stepped on a skylight and it broke."

My stomach clenched into a tight ball. Time slowed and my brain felt numb. I tried to concentrate on my sister's voice.

"He's at UCLA Medical Center now, and I believe he's being operated on. Mama and Daddy are there. I stayed home to try to reach you. I finally got hold of the people staying in your house and they gave me this number."

I felt like a thirsty sponge soaking in the information but, at the same time, like I was being wrung out.

"Lindy, all I know is that he has a skull fracture and they already had to remove his spleen but I know you can live without one of those."

What am I going to do? I'm in Spain. Ryan is in California. How long before I can get to him?

Ryan had dropped us at the airport just a few days before.

My warm and wonderful twenty-four-year-old son had wrapped his arms around me and bent over to give me a good-bye kiss on the cheek.

It was nice not to worry much about him anymore. He'd finally graduated from Pepperdine and landed a job as a production assistant on a TV show—maybe the first rung on the ladder toward becoming a writer for television and film. And he had just proposed to the love of his life. Ryan was ready to be a grown-up and take care of a family of his own. Now this!

It can't be happening. He has to be all right.

I have to get home.

Mike had woken up, heard my panicky voice, and wandered in to find out what was going on. Tyler, too, was now sitting up on his sofa bed. After I hung up, I told them that Ryan had had an accident and then we joined hands in that little living room and prayed, pouring out our fears to God.

As we held hands, my mind raced. I didn't know the details, so I could only guess at how bad Ryan's condition really was and what exactly I should be praying for. *A skull fracture? What exactly does that mean? Is that always terrible or do people get better from that?*

It was a mother's nightmare—the worst thing that had ever happened to one of my children and I was too far away to be able to get there quickly. Yet somehow I knew that God was with my son and that I would have to connect to God to be able to connect to Ryan. I have never been so grateful for the gift of prayer. When we called out to God, it didn't feel like a feeble ritual but rather a powerful intervention.

Maybe God would heal Ryan—but I had no guarantees. Maybe the doctors could keep him alive and make him well—but I really didn't know. All I did know was that God loved Ryan, God was with Ryan, and God was with the doctors.

As we stood together in that dark room in Spain, I prayed my heart out. "Lord, please surround Ryan with your love and let him live and recover from this awful accident. Help us get the plane flights we need to get to him as quickly as possible. Guide the doctors, nurses, and every human being who has something to do with Ryan's care."

After we said amen, we started hashing out our plans. Mike suggested waiting until we had more specifics on Ryan's condition. "Maybe it isn't so bad," he said. "Maybe Ryan will be safe in the hospital recovering and there is nothing we can do anyway if we go home. It can't be that bad that we can't hang here for a while. Maybe we shouldn't jump to conclusions."

But all I could do was tell Mike I was leaving. "You and Tyler can stay, but I *will* be on the first flight home." When he heard my voice, Mike quickly started packing too. He knew that even if Ryan was okay, I would need his support until we knew exactly what had happened and what we needed to do.

Mike took the lead in handling the logistics. After he'd spent an hour on the phone arranging for our tickets, we quickly packed, checked out, and headed for the airport. Then we began an agonizing twenty-four-hour journey on three separate flights—from Málaga to Madrid, from Madrid to Miami, and then a final flight home from Miami to Los Angeles. Each time we landed, I found a pay phone and called Debby. Each time I talked to her, I realized more and more that Ryan's life really was at stake.

The longest leg of the journey was the eight-hour flight across the Atlantic. Up to this point I was both numb and agitated, but I hadn't really absorbed the news. Now it began to sink in, and sitting still on that long flight got harder and harder. I felt impatient as time crept past.

Then I sat up straight. *I know what I can do. I need to write. I need a pen and paper so I can write everything I'm feeling. And if I don't, I'm going to explode.*

It took me a few frantic minutes to find a pen. Mike pulled some legal paperwork out of his briefcase, and I turned the pages over to write on the back. The words started pouring out and I wrote as fast as my shaky hand could write.

> *Trapped! It's a feeling of being trapped when you find out a child is hanging on the brink of life and death. Then to try to get to him, to be near him, tell him you love him, then to be on a plane, elbow to elbow with people who don't know and don't care and to spend hours and hours thinking he could have died and I wouldn't even know it—I'm doubly trapped! I want to scream and let the whole plane know I'M IN PAIN! I'M SCARED!*

I thought hard about what Debby had said in one of our calls. She told me doctors were having a difficult time getting a CAT scan of Ryan's head to determine the extent of the damage. He was on life support, and doctors were afraid that switching him to a portable unit in order to get a CAT scan was just too risky. That fact alone told me a lot about his condition, and the farther we got across the Atlantic, the more I awoke to a real, live, lasting nightmare. I was beginning to understand Ryan's situation and I knew the nightmare would not be over in a week or even a month.

I want to get home desperately, but once I do, I know I'm going to dread seeing him. Please, God, let him look like Ryan. I don't know how I'll react, and it matters to me that I behave in a way that will help him and honor him. If he can hear me, I don't want to scare him with my tears. I want my voice to comfort him.

As the news continued to sink in, I felt claustrophobic and then became very irritated at the people on the plane with us. They seemed blissfully unaware of my pain, acting as if all was right with the world. I watched them eating their prepackaged airplane food and laughing at the movie. As if there was anything to laugh about on this particular day! I knew I wasn't making sense but I felt as if I was on the verge of screaming.

My thoughts raced.

I want to be strong for Jessi and Tyler but I feel like I may fall apart and cause them more trauma.

I think Mama is trying to be strong for me. She must want to scream and crumble too. I know how she adores Ryan.

And the men—I feel sorry for Doug and Mike and Daddy. There's so much pressure on them to maintain composure. The women are expected to weep in front of the whole world but the men try to wait until it's private. Is it really easier for them to stay optimistic?

And Ryan's fiancée. Kristen.* What must she be going through? I feel a need to do and say the right thing for her. But what is that?

I wondered what had really happened. Was the sun in Ryan's eyes? Was that why he didn't see the skylight? Did he trip? Or did he think the surface was strong enough to bear his weight? I didn't know the details but my imagination stopped there. I couldn't allow myself to picture anything else.

I've given Ryan to God; I can imagine facing either a funeral or nursing Ryan back to health and then dealing with rehabilitation. But my absolute worst fear is serious brain damage. I've heard of brain damage where the patient has to relearn how to eat, talk, and walk. I can do that. But irreparable damage? I suppose I fear that the most.

✦ ✦ ✦

My parents live only five minutes from UCLA Medical Center, so my mother got there just as the paramedics who had transported Ryan from his building to the hospital were coming out of the emergency room. Mama went up to one of them and said, "That was my grandson. How is he?"

All he said was, "Lady, don't get your hopes up."

---

* Not her real name.

At this point, I was still asleep in Spain and unaware that my son's body had been broken. But Mama knew this was the start of a battle, and being a fighter, she rose to the occasion. As she always has. Mama has prayed for Ryan and for the rest of our family every day for as long as I can remember.

Mama waited for the doctors to fill her in on Ryan's condition. When the report came, it was all bad news. Ryan's lungs had collapsed from the impact. It wasn't clear how long he had gone without sufficient oxygen. Doctors had removed his spleen, which had burst, and he was still bleeding internally. Ryan's skull was fractured, and his jaw was broken. They suspected a spinal cord injury in the cervical column, and on top of everything else, he had a couple of cracked ribs and other serious internal injuries.

The doctors made it clear that people in Ryan's condition don't usually make it. Mama immediately called my father to inform him the accident was serious. He came down right away to join her.

Mama has always loved Ryan as if he were her own son. And somehow, what the doctors said didn't instill any fear in her. As my mother tells it, although she had clearly heard the warnings of both the paramedic and the doctors, she heard an even louder voice coming from within. All those years of studying the Word of God, committing those words to memory, and storing them in her heart had made her ready to clearly hear the Lord in Ryan's situation.

Deep down in her being she heard and knew this: *He will live and not die and declare the glory of God.* Mama felt no fear, shed no tears, felt the peace that passes all understanding, and knew this Word was from God.

Those twelve words from Psalm 118:17 are the reason Mama didn't experience fear when I would have collapsed in panic. I often wonder if, in the divine plan, I was placed halfway around the world from Ryan while my mother was just five minutes away because the need of the moment wasn't fear, but faith.

My parents sat in the waiting room and prayed, resisting fear whenever it threatened to rise up within them. Calls went out to family and friends, and the waiting room quickly became a gathering place for those who loved Ryan. Then our family began to try to reach us by phone. The only people who had the phone number to our condo were relatives of Mike who'd been house-sitting for us, and they weren't answering the phone. Several hours later, someone tracked them down and I finally got that middle-of-the-night phone call.

Ryan received thirty-six pints of blood over the next several hours as the medical team worked to stop the internal bleeding caused by organs hemorrhaging from the traumatic impact of the fall. Stopping the bleeding and getting Ryan on a respirator were the highest priorities right then. Later I was told that Ryan's heart stopped twice during their efforts to save his life. All the while I slept peacefully on the other side of the world.

As we approached Miami, I was in shock and grieving, but for a few moments I had some clarity as I caught a small glimpse of the days, weeks, and months ahead of me. Once again, I poured my thoughts out on paper:

I've often thought that something absolutely awful is bound to happen in my life. It's been too easy, too perfect. I know people grow through trials and struggles and I haven't had hardly any. I've almost felt guilty about it. But I've also wondered if it just wasn't my turn.

If it is my turn to grow and do something for the cause of Christ, then all I ask is, God, show me how. Don't let this suffering be for no reason.

CHAPTER 2

GROWING UP BOONE

In this culture, where entertainers and athletes wield
such power, it seems only right to me that they try
to make their influence a good one.

PAT BOONE

UNTIL RYAN'S ACCIDENT, I had very few problems. I grew up in a warm and nurturing environment. I enjoyed my teachers and my friends. I loved my sisters and my pets. My parents were loving but strict. I always wanted to please them and earned my reputation as a Goody Two-Shoes.

But there were times I got tired of being so good. Mama tells the story of a time she was talking over some issues with my older sister, Cherry, and my younger sister Debby. All of a sudden I burst into tears.

"What's the matter, Lindy?" My mom looked at me, worried.

"You're always helping the other girls with their problems," I cried, "and I don't have any problems!"

I've made up for it now, but as I look back on it, my childhood was charmed. We lived in a big house with a live-in housekeeper and cook—think Alice on *The Brady Bunch*. I was unaccustomed to doing laundry, cooking, or cleaning, but I never felt different from other kids. Although I grew up in Beverly Hills around celebrities and went to private school, I was raised to believe I was no different from anyone else.

My dad is a wonderful father. You've probably heard of him—Pat Boone, the teen idol in the V-necked sweater and white buck shoes with sixty-three hit records and three gold stars on the Hollywood Walk of Fame. Starting in the 1950s, Daddy was a big star and friends with people like Elvis Presley and Johnny Cash. He was known for drinking milk instead of martinis.

The woman behind the man was my mother, Shirley, a supermom who gave birth to four girls in three and a half years, who dressed us in matching, color-coordinated outfits, and who managed our family as efficiently as a high-powered corporate office manager. There was never a doubt that the four of us girls were her first priority, even in a town where many famous families pay more attention to their careers than their children.

Somehow while our dad was racking up gold records and starring in major motion pictures, both our parents kept us grounded with a firm foundation despite the wild and crazy currents of the entertainment business that swirled and raged around us. I'm not saying Mama and Daddy didn't make any mistakes or have any problems, but I grew up knowing family and faith were far more important than money and fame. I'm not quite sure how they did it, but maybe it had something to do with how they were raised.

Daddy's family had scraped by during the Depression, largely by raising their own food, including chickens, a few goats, and a cow, on a ten-acre plot of land outside of Nashville. My daddy remembers milking their one cow, Rosemary, while singing in the barn to help pass the time. Perhaps the family got some of their resourcefulness from their famous ancestor, Daniel Boone, the famous eighteenth-century frontiersman who blazed the Wilderness Trail through the Cumberland Gap of Virginia into Kentucky. Eventually, my grandpa, Archie Boone, began a small construction business, and Daddy remembers his father reading his Bible for an hour each morning before driving off in his pickup, a sign for Boone Construction Company painted on its side. Church was the center of life for the entire family, including my grandma, Margaret, and my dad's three siblings.

As a teen, Daddy was known around town for his outrageous sense of humor, Southern charm, and gentlemanly sense of courtesy. He started singing in church and then talent shows, often winning banana splits, the top prize in a weekly talent show at the Belle Meade Theatre in Nashville.

Then he was in a show that would change his life forever. When he was seventeen, he performed as "Discovery of the Week" in an outdoor concert in Nashville's Centennial Park along with Minnie Pearl and a country-western music star named Red Foley. Waiting backstage was Red Foley's daughter, a beautiful young girl named Shirley, who turned Daddy's head. "My heart took off double time at the sight of her," Daddy once said.[3] That girl would become my mother.

My grandfather, Red Foley, was a singer, musician, and radio and TV personality with two stars on the Hollywood Walk of Fame. A Grand Ole Opry veteran, he was a member of the Country Music Hall of Fame, and he sold more than 25 million records. He had a strong influence on the development of rock 'n' roll; Jerry Lee Lewis and Elvis Presley recorded many of his songs. He and his wife, Eva Overstake, had three girls. The oldest was my mama, who was named after Shirley Temple. Her mother dressed my mom like a doll and curled her hair into ringlets.

The three sisters recorded with their parents on Decca Records as the Little Foleys, but when Mama was just ten, her mother developed a serious heart condition and was in and out of the hospital. Mama and her sisters were separated a lot in those difficult years, and she needed something to hold on to. She found a Baptist church down the street and began to attend.

Mama remembers when her beloved aunt Connie (who was actually about her same age) was seriously ill with a ruptured appendix. At the Baptist Sunday school, my mom heard stories of the miracles performed by Jesus and she knew in her heart that God could save her aunt. Mama prayed, "If you will let Connie live, I will serve you the rest of my life. Dear God, I really will." Connie miraculously recovered from the deadly illness, so Mama decided to make good on her vow and was baptized. From then on, Mama felt a deeply personal connection to Jesus.

She needed that closeness with Jesus in the next few years as her mother grew more ill. The family lived in Chicago until she was twelve, then moved to Nashville, where my grandmother died five years later.

Although my parents had met before, Daddy and Mama really got to know each other when they both attended David Lipscomb, a high school affiliated with the Church of Christ. Before long they were inseparable. They decided to elope and were married by their high school principal, Mack Craig.

Mama and Daddy were just nineteen; they had very little money, and neither of them had a full-time job.

Mama got pregnant soon after with my older sister, Cherry (Cheryl Lynn). The new family moved to Texas, then New York City when Daddy became a regular on a national television program.

When Mama was expecting me, she faced a very serious situation—just six weeks before her due date, her doctor informed her that because of her Rh-negative blood type, her baby would most likely be born dead. She was grief stricken but tried her best to trust God. Not long after, at the Hotel Victoria on West 51st near Times Square, she went into labor four weeks early. As luck would have it, Daddy was away in Chicago for the weekend, and Mama was alone in the hotel room.

Daddy finally called her on Sunday evening to say he was on his way home. After Mama told him what was happening, he calmly asked, "Have you had anything to eat? Why don't you meet me at church and afterward we'll have dinner."[4] Mama was leaving the restaurant with Daddy when, right there on Broadway, her water broke.

I was born two days later, on October 11, 1955, at French Hospital. I was yellow with jaundice, but very much alive and an answer to Mama's prayers. My parents named me Linda Lee, but I've always gone by Lindy.

The next year Debby (Deborah Ann) was born, then Laury (Laura Gene). Four girls in three and a half years—pretty amazing!

At the same time that Daddy was trying to learn how to be a husband and a father to four little girls, he was taking a full load of university classes, making records, and hosting his own television show. Beginning in 1957, *The Pat Boone Chevy Showroom* was a half-hour variety show that aired on ABC. During those first four years of parenthood, my parents were busy doing much more than just changing our cloth diapers and mixing up bottles of formula. In addition to his other commitments, Daddy was a full-time student at Columbia University, studying to be a teacher. He was also making records for the label Dot Records. In the year I was born, he cut two gold records: "Two Hearts" and "Ain't That a Shame." Those were the first of a total of ten gold records he made in New York City.

He also filmed several major movie musicals including *Bernadine* (with Janet Gaynor), *April Love* (with Shirley Jones), and *Mardi Gras* (with Christine Carère and Tommy Sands). A national Pat Boone fan club was formed in Nashville, and Daddy received hundreds of fan letters every day. From 1955 to 1959, he and Elvis Presley were the only male solo artists to remain in the USA Top 100 without interruption.[5] When Daddy graduated from Columbia magna cum laude with a degree in English in 1958, *TV Guide* featured him on the cover in his cap and gown.

On the last episode of his TV show in June 1960, viewers were told that our family was moving to Los Angeles that summer. There's a famous photo of all six of us boarding TWA Flight 7 out of Idlewild Airport in Queens, headed for Hollywood. Cherry was six, I was four, Debby was three, and Laury, two. Mama dressed us in matching outfits. The photo shows Daddy wearing a straw hat, tilted and jaunty, and he's waving. Mama is beautiful. We look picture perfect, four little girls and a parent on each end, holding hands. So many celebrity families have carefully cultivated images with family activities staged for the camera and distributed to fans, and we were no different.

Because of Daddy's fame, we grew up used to lights, reporters, and camera lenses. Our every move was recorded and tracked. Fans could buy a Star Map and drive by our house in Beverly Hills. And most of the major events of our lives have been public.

The first Beverly Hills house we lived in was a world away from Daddy's early days milking Rosemary the cow. Our new rented mansion had marble floors, a grand staircase, and statues. It might not have been the best place for four little girls; Mama and Daddy ended up stringing chicken wire fencing along the high balcony to help keep us safe. Daddy loved the house and would've bought it, but at the time it wasn't for sale. Later, we learned that the next tenant was none other than Elvis Presley.

We moved several times until my parents found the perfect house—a two-story traditional white house with black shutters and a brick driveway. The grounds, which had big hedges for privacy, also included a garage for Daddy's cars and a big backyard with a pool, a lush side yard with a tiki hut playhouse, and a swing set. As you can imagine, I didn't spend much time in my room.

Early on, I think because of the media spotlight on our family, my sisters and I were given distinct roles when our parents talked about us in interviews. My older sister, Cherry, was the intellectual one, a straight-A student. She was also usually described as mature, super-intelligent, and a deep thinker. My younger sister Debby stood out because she was blonde, feminine, and adventurous. Later on, she developed into an extraordinary singer. Laury was the baby of the family, athletic, and a bit of a tomboy. And me? I was considered the "domestic" one, who liked to sew and just wanted to get married and have children, no career. I had dark hair, dark eyes, and a quiet voice. Daddy described me as direct, trustworthy, a conscientious hard worker, and "just good."

I tried my best to be a little bad, though. I was mischievous and loved to play Truth or Dare with my sisters and later, my friends. We'd dare each other to run through the neighbors' backyards without getting caught, play doorbell ditch, or make prank calls using silly accents. We loved to roller-skate up and down the driveway, and when that got old we put a long leash on our German shepherd and coaxed her into pulling us around on our roller skates by throwing a tennis ball in front of her.

Sometimes Mama could get a little over the top—for a while she had a mini roller coaster set up in our backyard and we loved it—one little dip, up and down, then we landed in the grass. We lived on the swing set and the slide, and when we became good swimmers, we pulled the metal slide over to the side of the pool and made our own waterslide.

One of my favorite things to do outside was explore the jungle. Well, at least that's how I thought of our side yard with its overgrown trees and bushes. In the jungle was a playhouse with a thatched roof that looked like a jungle hut. There was a main floor with a couple of tiny chairs, then a ladder up to a loft where there was enough room for two of us to lie down. It was quiet, peaceful, and a good place to think or read when we weren't using it for a jail in some of our more rambunctious games.

I might have been quiet sometimes, but I also loved to run around the backyard and scream, with Daddy chasing us in a game we called Monster. Daddy was the monster and we had to run away and get to home base. Daddy was young and energetic and always in great physical condition, so when he was around we had a blast playing with him in the backyard and in the pool.

Buses of celebrity seekers rolled slowly down our street with people looking up at our house, trying to catch a glimpse of one of us. When I was a tween my parents gave me a German shepherd puppy that I named Shep, after a famous song by my grandfather Red. One sad day Shep escaped through a hole in the gate and ran out into the street, where he got hit by a car. The neighbors called to let us know and Mama, my sisters, and I ran out into the street.

Shep was beyond help, and I was in too much shock to cry. Debby, however, fell to the ground and sobbed. Mama had us all gather around to pray for Shep. Daddy came out front to see what was going on, and just then, a busload of tourists pulled up and stopped to watch a Boone family drama as we huddled over the dying dog. Being a famous family means life on a stage. It's pretty hard to escape.

✦ ✦ ✦

It might seem strange, but so much of the Hollywood way of life didn't mean anything to me. I don't remember Elvis Presley, although he and Daddy were friends. Supposedly we bumped into him at an airport once and I'm also told he dropped by the house now and then. I guess the King didn't impress me that much; I was far too young to fall under his spell. I do remember the Beatles. Daddy took us to one of their concerts when I was eleven or twelve. I screamed my head off the whole time just because everybody else did, but I didn't really know why. We went backstage and met the Fab Four, including Paul McCartney, whom I swooned over. In fact, I couldn't think of anything to say to him. Laury wasn't as shy and sat on George Harrison's lap. Daddy was comfortable, as usual. He can carry on conversations with anyone and had no problem being at ease in the Beatles' dressing room. After all, he had his own stadiums filled with screaming fans.

Daddy also introduced us to teen idols like Fabian and Bobby Sherman, but I always felt a little awkward and didn't quite know how to act. To this day, I'm still starstruck, although I know this surprises people because of the environment I grew up in. Even when Daddy was at the peak of his popularity, I was scared to the point of being speechless around teen idols, rock stars, or anyone from television or the movies.

That may be a bit surprising, considering the fact that, from the time I was about twelve or thirteen, I toured with my parents and sisters as Pat Boone and Family. My mother had taught us some songs for fun when we were driving in the car, and we loved learning the harmonies. Our voices blended nicely.

I loved being on the road with my family. We traveled around the world together for over seven years, performing shows in the summers and often missing a week of school here and there. In fact, my best memories of growing up Boone are of us singing and traveling together. Better than any accolades were the fun family times we had on tour, staying up late, eating, and laughing together. Daddy loved spending time with us and sharing his love of performing with us; he used to joke that when it came to boys, he wanted to keep us moving targets.

When I was thirteen years old, Daddy took the whole family on a concert tour of Japan with the Osmond family. The Osmonds, including Donny and Marie, weren't well known yet but they were on the brink of fame, making regular TV appearances on *The Andy Williams Show*. The Osmond Family/Boone Family tour was a big hit, and we set attendance records all over Japan.[6] And guess what? The Osmond kids' mother dressed them alike, just like Mama dressed the four of us alike.

Each of us girls picked out an Osmond brother to get to know better. I remember Debby had a crush on Jay, the drummer, and I liked Merrill, who played bass guitar and had a raspy, soulful singing style. Cherry and Wayne dated pretty seriously for a while. Our families had a lot in common and we were close friends for several years.

A typical family show started with Daddy singing several songs. Then he'd introduce Mama, who would come onstage to sing a duet. Then it was our turn. We'd each give our name and age. "I'm Cherry, and I'm fifteen." "I'm Lindy, and I'm fourteen." "I'm Debby, and I'm thirteen." "I'm Laury, and I'm twelve." Then Mama would pipe up, "I'm Shirley, and I'm tired!"

My sisters and I would sing a couple of songs on our

own, and then we'd all sing together as a family. Our brand of family entertainment was a big hit, and I think audiences could sense our close, loving family bond. We also performed on TV variety shows hosted by Flip Wilson, Dinah Shore, Mike Douglas, and Glen Campbell. We even performed on a Bob Hope TV special. Later my sisters and I recorded several albums as The Boone Girls and even won awards and charted some Billboard hits with "When the Lovelight Starts Shining through His Eyes" and "Hasta Mañana."

✦ ✦ ✦

After we returned home from another concert tour, my sisters and I began spending our days at the Westlake School for Girls. My parents wanted to keep us away from the distractions of the opposite sex; in fact, Daddy believed in instilling a sense of trepidation in boys who would dare to come around to ask us out.

At home, Debby and I shared a room because we were the two middle kids, just eleven months apart, and we got along the best. We had very different ideas about how to decorate our room, however. I kept everything simple and organized, and I liked bright, glittery posters with inspirational sayings. I drove Debby crazy when I taped a big, brightly colored poster of Jesus over the window. Debby's tastes were a little more bohemian. She was into rock music and she favored Jimi Hendrix and Cream posters, all hip and psychedelic. Daddy was slightly alarmed and thought this signaled a rebellious streak.

Debby was adventurous and creative, and liked attention. She once had a terrific shiner, all purple, yellow, and black, around her right eye. She told everyone she'd gotten in a fight at school. Daddy decided to take a picture of her and got an adorable snapshot of her holding a kitten up to her face and looking at the camera to model her black eye. Only years later did she admit to him that she used crayons to apply the color to her face to create a fake bruise.

I didn't like to get in trouble—I was more compliant and never wanted to be at odds with my parents. I was always nonconfrontational and don't ever remember being grounded. I was always upbeat and positive, and accepted my parents' authority. One thing Daddy was strict about was demanding respect from his children. If we got out of line, and especially if we sassed him, we could expect a stern reprimand.

Another thing Daddy and Mama were strict about was family devotions during breakfast. We had little Bible storybooks, we sang songs, and then we prayed together. I have a photo from a magazine cover that shows us in the living room seated on our matching blue velvet loveseats. Daddy has a big Bible open on a table, Mama is holding another open Bible, and each of us girls (in matching outfits, of course) are holding and reading little Bibles of our own. The headline reads "Pat Boone Tells How He Uses God to Keep His Family Together."

Looking back, I'm also grateful for our family's evening prayers. It was a time to sit together without distractions, take stock of the day, hear what was on each other's minds, and give our cares and concerns to our heavenly Father. Precious moments. Don't think we weren't a normal family, though. Not all prayer times were picture perfect; they sometimes took place in the midst of sisterly squabbles or during moments of tension between my parents.

As far back as I can remember, my family went to church Sunday morning, Sunday night, and Wednesday night. There was never a discussion about it. If church was happening, we were there in the second row at the Church of Christ in Inglewood, California. No matter how late my parents had been out the night before, we were up and in the car for the half-hour drive down the 405 freeway. We were usually about ten minutes late for the service, but we still marched up to sit in the second row. Running late is a practice I hate to admit I inherited from my father. Daddy is notorious for not being able to get anywhere on time, so during most of our drives to church we listened to my mother chastising my dad for not planning his morning realistically. Fifty years later, I now get the same lectures from my husband.

After every service, Pastor Bob Cannon stood out front to shake hands and mingle, and my dad always made it a point to give him a compliment on the sermon. One Sunday I decided to go against my shy nature and I shook the minister's hand and said, "Your sermon was so good this morning even *I* listened to it!" I was about nine or ten, and I don't remember what the sermon was about but it was the first time I really remember tuning in to what the man up front was talking about.

Up to that point in the service, my sisters and I would try our best to sit still and behave. We enjoyed watching Daddy try to stay awake. He could fall asleep easily, a skill he must have developed over the years of piling on school and family responsibilities while making records and doing television. He could catnap and then keep on going, so sitting still was an invitation to nod off.

My sisters and I uncovered some of his staying-awake secrets: he would either hold his feet a few inches off the floor, a subtle way to keep his body alert, or he would pull out his pocket knife and discreetly jab himself in the thigh for some instant alertness. If he started losing the battle and his eyes grew heavy, the girls and I would point it out to one another and start to giggle. But we always had to pull ourselves together so we didn't get in trouble.

Even with the distractions, I did eventually start to pay attention to why we were sitting there and I heard the Good News of Jesus Christ. Our Sunday school teachers taught us the stories from the Old and New Testaments, we sang a song that helped us memorize the books of the Bible, and I learned the truths that would help me much later.

Church was a big part of our lives but there was a bit of a disconnect during my first decade. My parents weren't as happy as the rest of the world thought they were. You can imagine the stresses on a marriage where the man you love is also adored by women all over the world. Daddy was out traveling half the year, in and out of town with a hectic schedule, while Mama was home raising four small children. I love that my parents put such a priority on faith and church, but I knew from living in the same house that there were sometimes bitter fights that ended with doors slamming and my mother driving off in tears. Sometimes I wondered if our family was going to split like so many of my friends' families—I remember thinking maybe they should. They didn't seem happy.

Both of my parents have written books that detail their own spiritual journeys. I can add that both of them changed and that this had a profound effect on my whole family. First, my mother opened up to the power of the Holy Spirit as she was introduced to the idea that the God who worked the miracles we read about in the Bible still works miracles and that the power of God is the same yesterday, today, and forever. Mama started to experience a more personal relationship with the Lord, which led to a supernatural love she began to express toward my father. It wasn't the sappy romantic love that brings two people together but a deeper, enduring, *agape* love that heals, forgives, and commits. My dad felt the power of it and responded by wanting the deeper and more personal relationship with Jesus that he saw in his wife's life.[7]

My mother's faith impacted me when I was about twelve. We had a live-in housekeeper named Eva, who suddenly left for an extended period of time. Mama told us Eva had gone to Missouri to stay with family because she had cancer and needed to try to get well. I didn't think much about it. My mother hired someone else and life went on.

But I do remember watching my mother fall apart when we got the news that Eva had died. I was shaken by Mama's reaction and by the reality of death. I knew about dying, but no one I knew personally had ever died. I remember my mother's weeping and grief. At night, I remember thinking, *Someday I'm going to die. Wow. Is there any way out of that? This death thing includes me.* I didn't want to keep thinking about it, but when the lights went out and I was trying to go to sleep, it was all I could think about.

I don't want to die, I thought. *Is there a loophole?* I'd comfort myself by reasoning that there was nothing I could do about it and it probably wouldn't happen for a long time, anyway. But the thoughts wouldn't stop. *One day it will happen to me. What will that be like? Will I really go to heaven? Or will I just stop existing? What if there isn't anything after this? Is what I hear in church for real? If so, then why am I so scared? And why is my mother so sad?* I'd exhaust myself and finally fall asleep.

But something happened to my mother between the time Eva passed away and the day her father, Red Foley, died. Mama loved and adored him. Shaken by Eva's death, my mother had started a sincere journey to knowing Jesus personally; not as a religious figure talked about in church, but as the Son of God who lived two thousand years ago, died, and was resurrected. She began to realize that God wants to make a difference in our daily lives while we are on earth and that our prayers are a supernatural force that causes change—of heart, emotions, and health. She learned that the words of Scripture are a foundation we can stand on and we can speak those words back to the Lord in our prayers.

Mama's faith walk transformed her, so that when her father died, her fear and grief didn't overwhelm her as they had following Eva's death. Instead, Mama knew that she would be reunited with her dear father, that this world is not our home, and that heaven isn't just wishful thinking. She exhibited a grace that taught me there is no fear in death when you know Jesus.

I wanted that assurance and told my mother I wanted to accept Jesus as my personal Lord and Savior. I was baptized in the Church of Christ when I was twelve years old and that settled it—I was now certain that heaven was real and that I wanted to go there. Even today I have no fear of dying. I love my life and want to live a long time. I don't want to lose my loved ones, but I learned that if I have to say good-bye to them here on earth, it won't be forever. I was very young, and my commitment came from a naive and immature girl, but it was sincere.

As I entered my teen years, my whole family experienced a spiritual renewal and began attending The Church on the Way with Pastor Jack Hayford. Beginning with my mother, as a family we discovered the power of the Holy Spirit and a renewed belief in the power of prayer to transform lives. We moved beyond recited prayers like "Now I lay me down to sleep" and began to pray throughout the day as needs arose. Personally, I grew to expect to have God's ear the moment I addressed him in prayer, and I learned to talk to God the same way I would talk to anyone else.

As our family became even more outspoken about the role of faith in our lives, Daddy began to share openly about his new walk in the Spirit. When Daddy talked, people listened. When he shared the Good News of Jesus Christ with anyone who was interested, he offered to baptize them in the swimming pool in the backyard of our house in Beverly Hills. He kept a jumpsuit ready and he baptized over three hundred people in our pool, including several celebrities such as Wilt Chamberlain. At one point we spent a month in Las Vegas, performing two shows a night at the Fremont Hotel. We rented Phyllis Diller's house, and Daddy baptized people in her swimming pool too.

As the Boone family became more open about our faith, we also took our share of criticism and ridicule. Daddy was often teased about drinking milk, going to bed early, and being such a strict parent. We once did a family performance at the Great Gorge Playboy Club in New Jersey, a luxurious eight-story resort overlooking a golf course. Hugh Hefner's resort had 650 hotel rooms and featured a cabaret theater, ballroom, restaurant, and several swimming pools (no, Daddy didn't get to baptize anyone in *those* pools). It was billed as a "family friendly" resort, although there were plenty of Playboy Bunnies around.

Daddy had accepted the booking on the condition that there were no restrictions placed on what we could sing. The wire services picked up the story and reported that we came on as a family and sang pop tunes and gospel songs. As you can imagine, Daddy took a lot of grief for that one.

One night during our concert series at the resort, Mama was tired and didn't feel like going to dinner, so Daddy, my sisters, and I dressed up and went to dinner in a beautiful restaurant at the resort. Some man stopped by our table, saw us all dressed up and looking older than we really were, and asked Daddy, "What's your wife going to think about you having dinner with four Playboy Bunnies?"

"These aren't Bunnies," Daddy replied. "They're Boonies."

CHAPTER 3

THE DOMESTIC ONE

Having a sister is like having a best friend you can't get rid of.
You know whatever you do, they'll still be there.

AMY LI

I KNEW GOD LOVED ME, but I also lived in a very judgmental and critical part of the country. Hollywood is all about sex appeal and looking good, and no matter how you live your life at home, you can't help but be affected by the emphasis on outward appearance. So while I was an entertainer's daughter and enjoyed performing with my family, I never felt particularly attractive. Actually, I always felt slightly overweight. At that time short skirts were really popular and I thought my thighs were big. The entertainment world is focused on appearances, so I started jogging with my dad to get in shape.

In high school I had a PE teacher who taught a tumbling class that I loved. In fact, I've thrived on being physically fit ever since. Daddy was always into healthy eating and insisted we learn to love salads and vegetables. With his emphasis on organic food, he was even a little ahead of his time.

My obsession with my thighs wasn't the only thing that made me feel insecure. I usually felt a bit ordinary and plain around my sisters. Whenever there was a boy around,

I felt he either noticed the tall, mature, and very pretty Cherry or the blonde, blue-eyed, and talented Debby. My older sister, Cherry, looked mature for her age, and when she was fourteen, she had a nineteen-year-old boyfriend. My parents didn't allow her to date but her boyfriend was allowed to visit.

Cherry excelled at school and brought home straight As most of the time. She was a perfectionist and driven, and if you are a perfectionist at dieting, you can die. She very nearly did, and later wrote about her intense struggle with anorexia in her bestselling book, *Starving for Attention*.

Debby was the only blonde, blue-eyed sister. She is beautiful and has always been naturally funny. She also had the strongest, clearest singing voice of all four of us. In 1977 she recorded "You Light Up My Life," a song written for the movie of the same name and originally performed by another vocalist. However, when Debby recorded it in the studio, she sang it to God. There was something special about that song and the way Debby sang it.

Debby's version quickly became successful, surprising everyone—it became the most successful single of the 1970s and beat out Elvis Presley's "Don't Be Cruel" as the longest-running number one song. "You Light Up My Life" is ranked number seven on Billboard's All Time Top 100 songs. Debby even won the Grammy for Best New Artist in 1977. Perry Como, Debby's godfather, once asked Daddy if he was jealous of Debby. "Of course not," Daddy replied. "I would say it's better than my own success."

I felt least competitive with my youngest sister, Laury, who was the most athletic of us all and a bit of a tomboy.

Overall, I felt overlooked by the opposite sex because my sisters, in my opinion, outshone me. I longed for something that set me apart.

I wasn't a star student in school. I worked hard and earned As and Bs. I did take up sewing in high school and made a lot of my own clothes and even some of our stage costumes. During this era, Hawaiian shirts were all the rage. Our family loved Hawaii, too, so I started making and selling Hawaiian shirts.

I did make some money singing and was able to buy my first car, a Pontiac LeMans, with my sister Cherry. This was unique—most of our friends came from well-to-do families and were given really nice cars at age sixteen. My parents wanted us to have the satisfaction of buying our own first car. The car couldn't be too expensive and two sisters had to share. When Debby and Laury were old enough to drive, they bought a Pinto station wagon together.

Although our family wasn't perfect, overall I admired the way my parents had provided for us so well spiritually, emotionally, intellectually, and materially, and I wanted to care for a family of my own in the same way. Instead of thinking about a career, I began to think of myself as a homemaker, a domestic young woman ready for the responsibilities of being a wife and mother. I just wanted to be in love, have babies, and raise my kids. I embraced my role as the domestic sister.

When I was eighteen, I graduated from high school and went to Pepperdine University in Malibu, purely because my dad was on the board there. Daddy joked that we could go to any college we wanted to as long as we could be home for dinner. I didn't have a major or a career in mind, so I enrolled at Pepperdine and continued to live at home.

The campus was beautiful and I loved being by the beach. I enjoyed driving my LeMans over Sunset Boulevard and along the Pacific Coast Highway. For a fairly sheltered teenager (at least by Beverly Hills standards), this seemed like great freedom. I felt grown up and excited about who I would meet, the young men I might date, and just what surprises might lie in store.

At the same time, I wasn't in a big hurry to grow up and take on responsibility for my own life yet. My thoughts were still mostly on meeting a great guy and setting up house with him, then living happily ever after.

And would you believe it? My mom met him first. She was going to a weekly Bible study at Hal Lindsey's house. Hal was an expert on Bible prophecy and the author of the best-selling *The Late Great Planet Earth,* a book about Revelation that had everyone talking. One evening Mama spotted a tall, good-looking guy named Doug Corbin there. When she found out he was a senior at Pepperdine, she told him about her freshman daughter, even though he was in a serious relationship at the time.

She also told Doug about her book and promised him a copy.[8] When she found out he was in a class with me, she told me to look for a tall, good-looking, athletic type. Then she handed me a copy of her book and asked me to give it to him.

Doug was tall, handsome, and a star relief pitcher for the Pepperdine baseball team. He was glad to get the book because he was in a spiritually hungry time and he wanted to learn more about God and the personal relationship that God wants to have with each of us. After that, I remember meeting him at the baseball field after practice or coming to watch him pitch during games. Our friendship blossomed quickly into romance.

But I pulled an amazingly lame move just after I'd met him. I had arrived at school, parked on a steep part of the campus, and got out of the Pontiac juggling heavy books, my purse, and who knows what else. In a hurry, I hit the lock button and slammed the door. Then I heard the engine running. *Oh no!* I looked in the window and saw my car keys— still in the ignition. I panicked. *What do I do? How do I get my door open?* I don't remember the details, but somehow Doug spotted me as he drove by. He stopped and came over to wait with me for the Auto Club to arrive. In the end, I remember thinking it was a great way to get to know him better and it gave him something to tease me about. The incident cost me almost a tank of gas by the time I got back into my car, but I figured it was money well spent.

Doug could have had any girl he wanted, so when he seemed interested in me, I fell hard and fast. I began to dream about starting a home of our own with him. I was very naive but felt quite grown-up when we started talking about getting married two months after we met. I was still just eighteen, but my feelings for Doug—and his for me—were very intense.

My parents asked us to slow down, not be in a hurry, and wait to see how things developed. They reminded me of how they had struggled for so long, partly because they married so young. We respected their wishes, and they allowed us to get engaged when I was nineteen. They again asked us to wait another year to get married. We waited what seemed like forever, and just after I turned twenty, we got married. On November 29, 1975, Pastor Jack Hayford performed our wedding ceremony at The Church on the Way. I wore a simple long-sleeved dress with lace insets, a long train, and a matching long veil. The church was packed, and Daddy choked up when he tried to sing "Father of Girls" at our reception at Sportsmen's Lodge.

Not long after, Doug and I went on a Holy Land tour. It was the second trip to Israel for me. The first had been on a tour with my family when I was sixteen. We had done a live TV special from the Holy Land and cut an album called *The Pat Boone Family in the Holy Land.* There's a funny cover photo of the six of us in striped robes that look like they were made in Old Testament times. But the album was not the only creative work I did in Israel. Four years later, while there with my new husband, I got pregnant. We hadn't planned on having children right away, but being young and impulsive, Doug and I passed on the birth control one night and I realized just how easy it is for a twenty-year-old girl to become a mother.

After the first three months of morning sickness, which of course happens at all times of the day or night, I thought being pregnant was a delight. I ate whatever sounded good, and for the first time since puberty, I didn't worry too much about calories. I was in awe of the sensation of the baby moving around inside me. I felt comfortable with my changing body and couldn't wait to meet this little person face to face.

Doug and I took natural childbirth classes and I determined I wouldn't need drugs to deliver my baby. After fourteen hours of intense labor, the medical team broke my water and the birth went along quickly. My first son, Ryan Patrick Corbin, was born on November 12, 1976. He weighed five pounds, thirteen ounces. I was twenty-one, and a young twenty-one at that. I was thrilled to be the first of my sisters to have a baby and the exciting role of mommy! For once, I was center stage. I felt a new sense of importance—a living person needed me, and I knew I was cut out for the job. *I can be good at this.* All of my dreams were coming true.

Daddy was absolutely thrilled to have a new little baby boy in the family. He had always wanted a son. I remember Daddy proudly wearing a big pin on his V-necked sweater that said "Congratulations! IT'S A BOY!" and flashing that famous pearly smile for the cameras.

Mama and Daddy were young grandparents, both just forty-two, and they quickly decided names like "Gramps" and "Grandma" were out and chose "Daddy Pat" and "Mama Shirley" instead. All of their grandkids and many family friends still use those names today. Daddy said he didn't really feel like a grandfather for a while. This surprised him and he felt a little bad about it. Daddy remembered as a boy sitting on the porch with his grandparents down in Florida, with Granddaddy puffing on his pipe and spinning Br'er Rabbit stories. Granddaddy had been *old,* not young, fit, tan, and energetic like Daddy.

But Daddy's feelings changed forever one day when Ryan was about nine months old and I drove him over to visit my parents. Ryan was in his car seat in the front (this was back in the day when babies could still ride up front) and when we pulled up to the house, I released the buckle on Ryan's harness. He pulled himself up, looked out the window, saw Daddy coming out to meet us, and his eyes lit up and he began to wiggle with excitement. "I felt a warm feeling inside," said Daddy, "because now he was seeing me and wanted to get to me. That feeling taught me what a grandfather feels like." After that, Daddy and Ryan formed a very strong bond. Ryan was a snuggler, and he loved hugging Daddy Pat and Mama Shirley and sitting in their laps.

Ryan was such a happy baby. I think he inherited my genes for uncomplicated positivity. Before his first birthday, I became pregnant again. Now I was a pro at this and excited that a brother or sister for Ryan was on the way. This was my new area of expertise—carrying a baby in my belly. And once again, I loved every minute of it, even though I was tired because Ryan still hadn't started sleeping through the night. I was never very good at letting him cry himself to sleep. Someone told me, "Lindy, all you have to do is let Ryan cry it out one or two nights. Once he realizes you aren't going to pick him up every time he cries, he will start going to sleep on his own." One night I decided to try this method because I was so tired from not getting enough sleep.

That's when I discovered that, in addition to being affectionate, Ryan was strong-willed. He also had a strong gag reflex, which ended the battle of wills between us pretty quickly. On the night I had decided to let him cry himself to sleep, he bawled and bawled while I listened, trying not to give in. Then I heard gagging noises and went in to check to see if he was okay. He'd thrown up all over himself and the crib, so I changed his clothes and the sheets. Then I left him alone again to cry. I struggled not to go comfort and hold him, but after he threw up the second time, I'd had enough. I decided I'd rather hold him in peace than keep doing laundry and cleaning up baby vomit. Ryan got his way but it wasn't so bad; I loved holding him and rocking him to sleep.

My beautiful baby girl, Jessica (whom we call Jessi), was born just seventeen months after Ryan. I invited my sister Cherry to witness the birth; because she had battled anorexia, I was hoping to inspire her not to fear getting pregnant and having a baby. (It must have worked—she has five kids!) I also invited Daddy to the childbirth because in his day, dads didn't get to witness the birth of their children. When I think of it now, it seems crazy because I am very modest. But at the time I was enthralled with having babies and I thought it would be wonderful for him to witness a baby being born at least once in his lifetime, so he was there for his granddaughter's birth.

With a one-year-old and a newborn at home, my life still felt heavenly. I was living my dream of being a mother and wife. I had everything I ever wanted. But I was about to discover that my parents had been right: marriage can be hard, particularly when a couple marries young.

CHAPTER 4

THE FAIRY TALE FRACTURES

Hope begins in the dark, the stubborn hope that if you just
show up and try to do the right thing, the dawn will come.
You wait and watch and work: you don't give up.

ANNE LAMOTT

My youth and lack of dating experience, along with the pressures of buying a home and being responsible for a family, took a toll on Doug and me. I got antsy, wondering if I had gotten married too young and should have dated other guys. I remember thinking, *Is this all there is? What did I miss by leaving college and getting married and having kids? I still feel like a child myself.*

I had my house, two kids, and a nice husband, and I'd accomplished the sum total of anything I had ever looked forward to. I foolishly had never looked beyond this point to think about how I envisioned life after getting married and having babies; my parents had tried to warn me but I hadn't listened.

Doug grew disillusioned with me; he felt restless and struggled with managing our finances and keeping me happy. He also struggled with being the son-in-law of a legend; he wanted to be known as Doug Corbin, not just as Pat Boone's son-in-law. And Daddy was not just a famous entertainer, but a famous Christian. He was a tough act to follow.

Doug had taken on some difficult jobs, too. His first job was teaching and coaching in underprivileged schools in southeast Los Angeles. After a couple of years he took a job in the record business and became a junior executive in the Christian recording field.

Adding to our struggles and doubts was our sense that people around us were paying special attention to us simply because we were part of a high-profile entertainment family. Our youth, immaturity, and poor choices, compounded by media attention, led to problems. I was still performing with my family in concerts and on television. We filmed a pilot for a possible weekly TV show featuring guest stars and musical performances, along with Thanksgiving, Christmas, and Easter specials. Doug agreed to be a part of the first TV special but was very uncomfortable. He hated the outfit the costume department picked out for him; he didn't want to be part of our Partridge Family–type entertainment family and refused to participate in later TV specials. But I was enjoying the spotlight and felt disappointed that he didn't share my enthusiasm. There wasn't a lot of drama; we hardly fought at all and our day-to-day lives were mostly peaceful. But frustration and coldness and sadness crept in as we slowly drifted apart.

I began to wish I was single again. I wanted a time-out, not a divorce. Being so young and naive, I fooled myself into thinking I could live a single life for a while and get it out of my system, then reunite with Doug. I couldn't shake the feeling that I no longer wanted to be married. I liked going out with friends and wanted to be free. I was open with my mother about my frustrations and feelings and she said, "You know, Lindy, you've got a wonderful husband. You made commitments. You have two children. Don't play with fire. You'll destroy your marriage and family."

I told Doug about my feelings of restlessness, and we discussed a separation. Only then did I realize I'd been living in a fantasy world and really did want to make our marriage work. I began to find peace and satisfaction in our relationship again. Then one day Doug came home early from work. I was excited—this was one of the times our marriage seemed to be going well. *That's wonderful!* I thought. *It's the middle of the day and Doug's coming home.* Instead, he got very serious and told me he didn't love me anymore and that our marriage wasn't going to work out. I was blindsided. Then he left.

I was distraught. Ryan was two years old, Jessi was a baby, and I was twenty-three. I went home to my parents' house and they consoled me and helped with the kids. After a time, Doug and I got back together. We both believed divorce was wrong and we loved Ryan and Jessi and didn't want them to have a broken family. But it didn't work; we split up again. And that is how it went for the next few years—back and forth, together and apart, moving to a new house every time we got together.

The one time I felt hopeful was while listening to certain music. When I was worn out and longed to sense God's love, I played the song "Which Way the Wind Blows" by the 2nd Chapter of Acts. When I did, I felt as if God's Spirit was letting me know he was with me and loved me.

The lyrics reminded me that, just as I didn't know which way the wind was blowing, so I couldn't plan my future. During this time, my life seemed to change every six months.

I would be in a new job or a new home or just separated from Doug or just back together. This song reminded me that "Jesus knows which way the wind blows"[9] and I could give him all my tomorrows. I couldn't listen to the song without crying.

Each time Doug and I broke up and then reconciled, the emotional toll was more intense. When we would get back together, we would try to get along. I'd think, *This time we're going to be happy.* But after a while so much damage had been done that our marriage was fragile, like a china plate that has been glued together one too many times.

Finally, it ended. My seven-year-long fairy-tale marriage was finally over. I had been the first of my sisters to be a mother and now I was the first one to get divorced.

Not much to celebrate. I cried and mourned, both because I loved Doug and because my dream of a restored marriage had been shattered. But I didn't have the temperament to be down for long. Soon I dusted myself off and decided to try again for happiness.

Now, as I reflect back, I can only imagine your thoughts: *What an idiot! Surely you had the concept of godly marriage taught and modeled for you, along with premarital counseling. How could this have happened so early in your marriage?* All I can say is yes, I *was* an idiot. Life had been served up on a silver platter for me and it was all good. Being sheltered by my parents was a loving way they kept me from getting hurt as a teenager. Because I'd never challenged their rules while living at home, I'd never made bad choices and suffered the consequences there. I'm the kind of person who learns from making mistakes, but I'd been so sheltered that I almost didn't have the chance to make one. Once I got married and moved out, the cost of a bad choice was much higher, and somehow I didn't anticipate the pain I would cause my husband and young children.

Our marriage difficulties had been hard on my folks for many reasons, but largely because they adored Ryan and Jessi. My parents had formed a tight bond with my two kids, and their hearts broke because they didn't want them to be the product of a broken home.

They also extended their love to me. When I was forced to go to work, Mama offered to have the kids at her house in the summers so I didn't have to pay for child care then. (I took low-paying office jobs, and with two children, the child-care costs ate up most of my paycheck.)

Not only was I grateful to Mama for watching Ryan and Jessi, I loved seeing my kids happy and flourishing at the house I grew up in, swimming in the pool, playing Monster or basketball with my dad, and making up adventure games to play in the jungle hut. Ryan loved make-believe and he used to get in his Superman Underoos and pretend he was a superhero while my dad was the bad guy who chased him around. Ryan loved it.

Every time I brought Ryan to my parents' house, he would run at full speed from the entryway to the kitchen, and then jump down the two stairs that separated the dining room from the den, where my parents usually hung out in their favorite easy chairs.

My mom remembers Ryan frequently coming to sit on her lap and ask questions about God. She taught him how to get on his knees by his little rocking chair and pray.

Daddy taught Ryan (and all of his grandchildren) three things to remember, and he always made the kids repeat them: "One, my parents and grandparents love me. Two, Jesus loves me. Three, I'm a good boy." He wanted to build a strong self-concept to help them get through hard times—something my kids needed early on.

Ryan especially loved going with my parents to their house in Hawaii, where he'd golf with my dad or pick bananas off the trees to make banana pudding with my mom.

+ + +

As a single, working mom, I had a busier life than before. Being a mom was the most important thing to me; I adored my two children and gave them a lot of my time. I was constantly making lists, budgeting time and money, and trying to carve out an hour for exercise each day.

No matter how busy I was, I made time for two things that kept me feeling and looking good. I get both of these priorities from my dad, I'm sure. I always made sure I worked out, and I always tried to find time to be in the sun. Exercising is a great habit. But tanning is pure vanity, and I now know it's not good for me. In my teens, getting tan helped clear up my skin and I thought it made me look thinner, too. I'd go to great lengths to find a little sun time.

Here's an example of my warped priorities at the time: When I worked as a receptionist at a law office in Newport Beach, I used to wear my bathing suit under my work clothes. At lunch, I would take my bag lunch up to the roof, where I kept a folding chair. I'd get down to my bathing suit, eat my lunch, relax, and close my eyes for a bit in the sun. When lunch was over, I'd get dressed again and go back to work. And that's how I maintained my year-round tan. Cut me some slack—I was still in my twenties!

With all of the upheaval surrounding the separations, the divorce, and going to work, my relationship with God was pushed to the back burner. Because of my busy schedule, I didn't go to church as often as I felt I should. While I'd never missed a Sunday when I lived with my parents, when I was out on my own, I discovered the sky wouldn't fall if I skipped a service—so I frequently did. I didn't prioritize my prayer life either.

That's not to say I ever doubted the existence or majesty of God. I remember telling a friend once that I had to believe in God because I didn't see how the tail of a peacock could possibly have come into being randomly. When open, the pattern and iridescence of the tail's purple, teal, green, and blue feathers are simply too beautiful and orderly. No matter how strong or weak my connection with God, I have always stopped to stare at the vibrant colors of a peacock, a rainbow, or a sunset. The beauty of their design speaks to me of a Designer. I could never deny that.

But while I trusted that God was near, I didn't spend much time with him and I wasn't living a consistent, faith-filled life. I continued to rely on the foundation of faith that had been built by my parents.

And while I still loved God, I wondered if it even mattered whether I lived a Christian life. After all, I'd married a Christian and in the end had tried to make our marriage work—only to fail miserably. Once Doug moved out, I was so hurt and felt so rejected that I took whatever positive attention I could get. That meant I dated when I should have waited. More and more I began to live the way of the world. I felt distant from God, and though I still found hope in the thought of heaven, it felt distant and irrelevant to my life just then.

I faced temptations and sometimes I gave in. I would feel bad and I believed in a forgiving God, so I never felt like he gave up on me. Sometimes I didn't understand what was going on in my own heart and mind. When I knew I wasn't living my life the way I should, I would practically argue with God: "I don't understand what's going on. Why all the temptations? I can't help what I feel. It's the way you made me."

I felt like I had a constant craving for love and for meaning that was never satisfied. I know the Lord heard my heart's cry. I wanted to live consistently. I wanted to be close to him again. I prayed that he could put my life back together so I could live in a way that was pleasing to him.

Once again, I know that heaven heard my desperate pleas, and I felt the Lord using one particular song to woo me back to himself. This time it was Keith Green's song "When I Hear the Praises Start."[10]

This song absolutely slayed me. I was divorced, so I felt like the black sheep of the Boone family. Yet through its lyrics, Jesus was saying, "I did it all when I was dying. . . . I see no stain upon you." This song enabled me to turn my face back toward God, and every time I played it, I felt cleansed and hopeful I could have a chance at a fresh start.

I am amazed as I look back and consider the patience God extended to me and his constant willingness to be near when I cried out to him, even when I had moved closer, only to drift away again. Many times I lost my connection with heaven because I turned away from God, but every time I turned back to him, I discovered that he hadn't gone anywhere. His message was the same; I could count on it: "I love you. You are forgiven."

✦ ✦ ✦

During my time at the law office, I met an attorney named Mike Michaelis. We had a few casual elevator conversations and he'd smile at me as he passed by my desk. Finally he asked me out for a drink. I didn't care for alcohol, so our first date was spent over iced tea at Carl's Jr. We had fun talking and laughing. Afterward, Mike went back to the office and told his attorney friends, "Just my rotten luck—she's Pat Boone's daughter!" Mike liked me but he remembers thinking, *This is never going to happen. I've always been on the other side of the Boone lifestyle.*

But surprise, surprise—I liked Mike. I liked him a lot. He was smart, funny, good-looking, and a hard worker. In fact, he often worked sixty to seventy hours a week, and sometimes on the weekend. He specialized in auto dealer law, and in addition to his casework, he traveled around California teaching workshops and seminars.

Every few weekends he would take off to go snow skiing at Mammoth Mountain or water-ski down at the river to get away from work pressures. Back in those days, not everyone expected you to keep your cell phone with you at all times, so it was easier to unplug and enjoy being away from work.

Of course, once we met and started dating, I helped him with that!

As I got to know Mike, I found out that he'd studied criminology in college and he'd always wanted to be an FBI agent. His upbringing had been very different from mine. His father had been in law enforcement, but his parents had divorced early on and Mike never got to spend much time with his dad. His father was distant and didn't even pay child support. His mother moved in with Mike's grandmother and after a while, his mom began dating and moved out and got her own apartment, leaving the kids with her mother. Mike's mom eventually remarried and Mike and his sister stayed with his grandmother.

Mike's grandmother was a strong woman who worked forty hours a week on the assembly line at the General Electric plant in Ontario, California, making electric irons. She worked there for forty-three years and served as the union steward, advocating for the other employees. Mike took after his grandmother in her strong sense of justice, work ethic, and stubbornness, and early in life he understood that he was going to have to fend for himself. He grew up tough, strong, and independent, and he vowed that if he ever got the chance, he would be a very different father from the one who had been mostly absent from his life. Mike always wanted to be a good provider like his grandmother.

We fell in love and I began to think about making a life with Mike. There was just one thing that made me nervous—he wasn't a Christian. Every once in a while growing up he'd go to church with a friend. And his grandmother occasionally went through religious periods where she'd make Mike and his sister go to church, mostly at the local Baptist church, where his biggest struggle was trying to stay awake.

He wasn't an atheist, because he was smart enough not to rule out the possibility that there was a God out there somewhere. But he was definitely agnostic; he just didn't see the point of a personal relationship with God, and the Bible seemed to be an interesting historical and philosophical book but nothing much more than that.

As we began to think about marriage, I knew I wouldn't be marrying a believer. I didn't go into the marriage with some big plot to convert him. "She never pressured me," I've heard Mike tell our friends. "She let me exist and carry my own thoughts." I loved him for the wonderful man that he was. But in my heart of hearts, I also felt a little on the outs with God because I was thinking about marrying someone who wasn't a believer and who walked such a different path from that of my mom and dad.

My parents didn't approve and wanted me to reconcile with Doug. While I was torn, I felt very disillusioned because my marriage to a Christian hadn't worked out. I loved Mike's strong sense of responsibility and generosity. I liked his friends and his family. He was funny and mischievous, and had a big heart—a good clue was his love for the Disney channel, along with the four little stuffed animals he kept on his bed. So I left his salvation in God's hands and I tossed the dice. I loved him and hoped for the best.

Although we had a strong attraction to each other, we moved slowly. Though he'd been married once before, Mike had no children and wasn't quite sure he was ready to be a stepfather. His family had been splintered and scarred by alcoholism, remarriages, and difficulties with stepparents. He knew what bad stepparenting was and he had a vision for what a good stepparent would look like, but he knew it wouldn't be easy and wasn't sure he wanted to take it on.

After we had dated for about eighteen months and he still hesitated at committing to a long-term relationship with me, I let him off the hook and told him I would have to move on. "I must not be what you are looking for," I remember telling him.

"Would you leave the door open a crack while I try to work this out?" he asked.

Mike decided to go to a counselor to figure out why he was having such a hard time committing to me. One obvious reason was that since he and I had both been married before, he wanted to be sure that if he married again, it would be forever. I liked that about him. I knew if he ever did ask me to marry him, I had found someone willing to work through the tough spots.

But I was really surprised to find out that one of the reasons for Mike's hesitation was that he had problems seeing himself as a stepfather to Ryan. I was taken aback because in my mother's heart and mind, Ryan was a sweetheart. *What's not to love?* Mike saw it differently.

Mike loved adventure and the outdoors. He owned a ski boat and spent a lot of time on the Colorado River water-skiing. He also enjoyed snow skiing and offered to teach my kids. My daughter, Jessi, could pick up anything athletic and be pretty good at it right away. She never had any fear of trying anything new. "Jessi is the kind of kid I understand because she is gutsy. She'll try anything," Mike said.

But Ryan was different. He had been a tiny baby but had grown up tall and skinny. His feet turned inward and got in his way, and he just didn't catch on to athletic things as fast as his sister. Ryan didn't enjoy amusement park roller coasters, and he didn't even seem to like the beach because he didn't like sand getting all over his clothes or his skin. He always wanted to please so he would try something if it wasn't too scary, but he often opted out of activities that involved high rates of speed, so water-skiing terrified him. Mike insisted he at least try it and he was frustrated at Ryan's unwillingness to take chances.

Even Ryan's own father, Doug, thought Ryan's personality was almost too much like mine—happy, positive, innocent, and not at all tough or adventurous. And as an experienced athlete, Doug always worried about his son and felt that Ryan needed some toughening up.

To Mike, Ryan was soft and timid and a bit of a mama's boy. As I write this, I can see how Mike got this impression. He was reacting to a real part of Ryan's personality at the time. Just the year before I met Mike, when I was a single mom, I had a dinner party at our house. I was in the kitchen cooking and cleaning up while others were laughing and relaxing in the living room. Ryan, about six at the time, was hanging out with me in the kitchen. I finally said to him, "Honey, everybody is in the other room. Why don't you join the party?"

"Because I don't want you to be alone," Ryan said.

His small comment remains with me still. I remember feeling so blessed. *Where does this kid come from? Why is he so sweet and why am I so lucky?* Ryan has never been afraid to show love, and even better, to voice love. While he might have shied away from roller coasters and water skis, he was never afraid of loving abundantly. He had a tender heart and he was never embarrassed to show it, no matter who was around.

Ryan's loving personality extended to people he had never even met. He reminded me of my dad. For eighteen years, Daddy was the national spokesperson for Easter Seals. He raised hundreds of millions of dollars for people with all kinds of disabilities and challenges, and he hosted their annual telethon to raise money for Easter Seals. At that time telethons were popular and got huge ratings. Ryan watched and some of the stories must have touched his heart.

"Can I help?" he asked me when he was just four years old. "Can I take something to the kids?"

"You have some money in your piggy bank," I said. "But you've been saving up to go to Disneyland. Would you rather give it to the Easter Seals kids?"

"Yes, Mommy."

I decided to take him down to the studio so he could give his piggy bank to his Daddy Pat on his own. When we arrived, there were just two hours left in the telethon. Numbers were mounting as the producers broadcast short films of people overcoming obstacles. Then Ryan climbed the steps and walked across the stage holding his piggy bank. Daddy came unglued and his eyes filled with tears. "That was so typical of him," Daddy says. "That was all he had to go to Disneyland and he brought it to help kids he didn't know. That was Ryan."

Ryan and Jessi had my heart and were precious to me.

But for some reason, when Mike openly and bravely shared his concerns with me, I didn't become irate and say, "Just move on! I'll find someone who likes my boy more." Instead, I reacted with calm confidence. In my heart I knew there wasn't a thing in the world wrong with Ryan. After all, he had only been seven years old when Mike came into our lives.

I believed in Ryan and that as he grew he would become braver and more willing to try new things. I just knew he would try new sports and experience adventures and that he would find something to be good at. Even more important, I knew that Ryan was a good person, a loving and caring human being, and that I would never want to change him in the least. As Mike spent more time with Ryan, I was sure that he would see the amazing soul developing in that skinny, awkward-looking body and that he would love him just as I did. So I assured Mike that this wouldn't be an obstacle to our having a good life together.

After we had dated for about a year, I took Mike to get to know my parents. We were both a little nervous because Mama and Daddy had made their disapproval known about their daughter dating an unbeliever. We had a pleasant, casual visit, but before we left, they said they wanted to pray for us. They got down on their knees and prayed. I remember wondering what Mike was thinking when they started praying aloud fervently. But it didn't scare him off, and after two years of dating, we married on Christmas Eve of 1985. Ryan was nine, and Jessi was seven.

Slowly, a strong, loving bond grew between Mike and his stepson, Ryan, and his stepdaughter, Jessi. Mike respected Doug and never tried to take his place with the children;

instead, Mike tried to be a provider and gave help wherever he could.

Two years later, our son Tyler was born. Six and a half weeks before my due date, I went into intense labor. We called our closest friend who lived nearby, Mike's business partner Bill Lowrey, to keep Ryan and Jessi while we rushed to the hospital. Tyler came so fast that I almost gave birth in the car! Mike felt a little cheated because he didn't get to coach me through labor.

When we called Bill with the news that I had just given birth to a healthy baby boy, he told the kids. Ryan broke down and cried. He seemed able to feel things at a deeper level than I would have expected for an eleven-year-old boy.

After Tyler was born, Mike made it a point to attend Ryan and Jessi's school events and work a bit less so he could spend more time with the children and me. Our blended family grew close as love knit our hearts together. And little did Mike know that in the years ahead, his stepson Ryan would have a profound impact on his spiritual journey.

CHAPTER 5

HANDY AND THE CAN-DO KIDS

You've got to jump off cliffs all the time
and build your wings on the way down.

RAY BRADBURY

RYAN HAS ALWAYS wanted to make movies and TV shows. Maybe that's because he grew up in a showbiz family in the entertainment capital of the world. He always loved spending time with my parents and had great fun watching Daddy Pat's movies. A favorite memory was taking Ryan and Jessi to watch Daddy film a guest role on season four of *Moonlighting*, a hot television series starring Cybill Shepherd and Bruce Willis as sparring detectives. Daddy played a dream version of David, Bruce Willis's character.

Or maybe Ryan loved the idea of creating stories because he was artistic in his own right and had something important to say. When he was about eleven, Ryan started drawing comic book characters. He loved collecting Captain America and Superman comic books, and at first he tried to draw freehand the characters on the covers. But soon he came up with his own idea for a comic book series featuring a disabled superhero, Handy and the Can-Do Kids. He probably still had a heart for the Easter Seals kids and he wanted to make them feel better. He noticed that kids with disabilities don't have any superheroes that look like them.

The main character was Hanford, nicknamed Handy. His parents had been killed in a car accident, and Handy had been left a paraplegic in a wheelchair. At the hospital where he went for rehabilitation, Handy met other kids who had special abilities. There was a blind kid with supersensitive ears, a quadriplegic with Stephen Hawking–like intelligence, a deaf kid with X-ray vision, and Happy, a kid with Down syndrome who had super strength. Handy had a supernatural imagination, and whatever he imagined would materialize out of thin air. If the bad guys were trying to escape, Handy could imagine a brick wall across the road and the bad guys would crash their car into it. Handy also had a special flying wheelchair equipped with ray guns. In the first Can-Do Kids story, the group broke up a drug gang.

When Ryan was twelve, he wrote up a treatment for a pilot and Daddy arranged for him to meet with Joe Barbera of Hanna-Barbera, which produced shows like *Huckleberry Hound*, *The Flintstones*, *Yogi Bear*, *The Jetsons*, *Scooby-Doo, Where Are You!*, and *The Smurfs*. Ryan carefully packaged up his drawings and notebook, and he put on a tie for the big meeting. Joe Barbera welcomed Daddy and Ryan into his office and sat them down. "Tell me about your idea."

Ryan told him the story of Handy and the Can-Do Kids. Mr. Barbera thought for a moment, then said, "I really like this idea. We can do it at Hanna-Barbera animation, but we'll need a quarter of a million dollars to shoot the pilot." Well, we didn't know where to get funding for an animated series so the project never got off the ground. But I treasure in my heart the thought of my son spending the time to create a superhero story to encourage other children. And I couldn't have guessed that, in a few years, the story of the hero in the wheelchair would take on a whole new meaning for me.

As Ryan, Jessi, and later Tyler reached their teen years, I enjoyed watching them go to football games and school dances, as well as seeing them get all dressed up for prom pictures. Neither Ryan nor Jessi was quite the Goody Two-Shoes I was, and I appreciated their adventurous spirits. Sometimes they broke curfew or other minor house rules and got in trouble, but overall I loved that they were just normal teenagers making mistakes, learning from them, and experiencing life in a way I never did growing up in a more protective household.

As Ryan got older, he often did skits or lip-synched songs at school events. In sixth grade he ran for student body president and won, and was elected again in eighth grade. He had no fear of being up front and enjoyed the feel of a microphone and all eyes on him.

He still wasn't superathletic, though. Once Jessi and Ryan competed in a footrace around the backyard of my parents' house and Jessi beat him. Can you imagine being a big strong teenage boy and having your little sister beat you? Not only that, but she outdid him with waterskiing and snow skiing. Jessi was quite the athlete and later won the state championship for Irvine High in cross-country. Even Tyler was more athletic than his big brother; he excelled at soccer and loved to play golf with Daddy Pat. "Tyler could be a pro if he wanted," Daddy always says.

But even though Ryan didn't show much early athletic

ability, he loved being part of a team. He grew tall and lanky. He played baseball like his dad; it was a struggle and didn't come easily but I did notice that he always checked to see if his dad and I were watching him. He wanted to make us proud. One day he hit a big home run for his Little League team. His teammates circled around him to jump up and down and celebrate as he rounded home base and the local newspaper published the picture. He notched about five home runs that season and had his first taste of athletic fame.

When Ryan was about fourteen years old, he finally found something he could excel at: basketball. He shot up in height right before his freshman year. His strength and the extra few inches gave him enough confidence to try out for the team, and he turned out to be especially good at rebounding. But it wasn't easy at first. His dad remembers going to one of Ryan's freshman games and finding him sitting on the bench.

"What's wrong? Why aren't you playing?" Doug asked.

"My toe hurts," Ryan said.

Doug had a feeling that it was fear, not an injury, that kept him on the bench. "He didn't yet have that attitude that 'I can overcome things,'" Doug once shared with me. "I was afraid he might get pushed around. I wanted to toughen him up a little bit."

So Doug told him to get back in the game. "Ryan, you tell the coach you can play. If it's not broken or sprained, tell the coach you can play, even if it hurts." Ryan did, went back in the game, and played well.

Even though Ryan was the big brother, Jessi felt like she had to watch out for him at times. They were opposites; she was a tomboy and liked to pick on him and boss him around.

But she also remembers talking to him about how to stand up for himself. They used to roughhouse sometimes, wrestling or having food fights when we weren't home. One day when Ryan was fifteen or sixteen, she pushed him too far and he lifted her off the ground and pushed her up against the wall. Jessi was scared for a moment, then thought, *Wow. There he is!* At that moment, she realized her brother was starting to grow into himself, find courage, and become more assertive.

Tyler adored his big brother and loved playing basketball with him, although Ryan towered over him. "He was the guy I looked up to the most," Tyler said. "He always talked to me and gave me a lot of attention." Tyler loved riding around in Ryan's white Mitsubishi Eclipse and listening to music. They played video games and became obsessed with Madden Football.

Ryan's confidence grew as he kept growing and putting on muscle, topping out at six-foot-four. He played basketball all four years at Irvine High School and made varsity as a junior in jersey number 32. He was scrappy, energetic, and diligent, and his effort energized the team. His senior year he was captain of the varsity team and voted Most Valuable Player. He also broke the record for most rebounds both in a single game average and in a season, holding those two records for many years.

Toward the end of his senior year at the final basketball banquet, Ryan took the podium to give a speech as captain and Most Valuable Player. As usual, he showed no fear at being up front. On this special night, Ryan stood tall, wearing a deep blue shirt and a brightly patterned tie, his hair brushed neatly straight back. He summed up what he had learned from the coaches and his teammates and then, in an emotional moment, ended by thanking his dad for everything he had taught him about and through basketball. Doug came up and gave him a big hug in front of everyone.

Ryan didn't make captain because he was the best player; he was made captain because he had heart. After graduating he went back and coached the freshman team, worked the games as announcer, and tried his best to give back to the school that had given him a safe place to try something new.

Ryan did have an awkward side and got teased because he was different—he had a sweet nature that seemed mostly devoid of rebelliousness. His friends teased him relentlessly, and years later, his sister bought him a birthday card that said he was the perfect mix of superhero and dork. We all agreed he was handsome, dear, and a little bit of a nerd. He always wore his heart on his sleeve and was too nice to be a bad boy, so he wasn't always that popular with the high school girls, although he did have a girlfriend his junior and senior years. Allison was his first love; she must've realized bad boys aren't all they're cracked up to be. Although they went their separate ways after graduation, Ryan bonded with her whole family. They loved him back, and still do.

He rarely got in trouble and if he did break the rules and disobey, it was usually to help someone else. One time he was out with a high school teammate who was upset because their basketball team had lost the final game of the season. They both stayed out past curfew and Ryan told us he was spending the night with his friend. I got a call in the morning from a police officer, saying they had my son. He'd been asleep in his car, his long legs and enormous feet sticking out the window. Both boys were busted—apparently it's against the law to sleep in a car near a school crosswalk. When I heard Ryan's typically noble reason behind the occasional wrongdoing, I couldn't get angry at him. When he had to be disciplined, he usually just accepted the penalty because he knew he had it coming. He was an easy kid.

When it came to college, Ryan wasn't the most organized guy in the world. His grades weren't bad but they weren't that great, either, and he didn't get any scholarship offers to play basketball. He had a few friends who planned to attend a certain college, so Ryan applied to just that one school and was shocked when he wasn't accepted. He didn't have a back-up plan, so he ended up at a junior college for a couple of years and took odd jobs ranging from DJing on the college jazz radio station to valet parking to announcing basketball games back at Irvine High.

He applied to Pepperdine University for his junior year and was accepted. I think he was motivated by the fact that Jessi had graduated high school and had already started at UCLA. That summer Ryan surprised me by doing something very adventurous: he took off on a trip to Europe with two buddies. My husband, Mike, funded the trip; I was amazed at his generosity, but he felt Ryan had earned it.

Along the way, the boys met some American girls in Prague, who invited the boys along on a crazy extreme adventure—bungee jumping off a dangling gondola in the Swiss Alps. At that time it was billed as the World's Longest Bungee Jump.

Gulp.

When the girls were in the middle of trying to talk the boys into joining them, Ryan told me he was thinking that bungee jumping was pretty far down on his life list, but he felt pressure—*How can I be the only one without the courage to do it?*

Ryan was into filmmaking at the time and documented every step of the trip; the video is a hoot to watch. Ryan's nervousness is palpable as they rode in the gondola all harnessed up. It didn't help matters that they were in the middle of a thunderstorm with rain pouring down outside. As the Stockhorn Gondola made its way over rocky cliffs with a waterfall, Ryan and his friends got ready to hurl themselves 450 feet through the air.

He did it. And I'm glad I wasn't there.

Afterward, his friend interviewed him on camera and Ryan was so excited, adrenaline pumping. "I was the guy who didn't want to do this," he said. "I was brought up not to do this kind of thing!"

Then he smiled. "We were supposed to dive and go head-first." As a kid Ryan had tried and tried to learn how to dive but at the last minute, he always jumped feetfirst. This time wasn't any different.

"I went out the door feetfirst. The rope wrapped around my arm. I looked over and said, 'I'm a dead man.' Then I went into a jackknife and did a reverse backward dive," he said into the camera.

"It was indescribable . . . total uncertainty and the most exhilarating thing I've ever done." His act of courage (or idiocy, depending on your point of view) changed the way Ryan viewed himself. It represented a giant step into manhood for him. And I was secretly glad that he had done it.

Later in the trip his friends ran with the bulls in Pamplona, Spain. Ryan sat that one out. He'd already proven he was no coward.

That summer trip to Europe changed Ryan. He came home stronger, more confident, and more grounded.

That fall he started at Pepperdine and majored in telecommunications. When we visited him in the dorm, Tyler was amazed at how friendly his big brother was, going up to strangers with "Hi, I'm Ryan."

"Did Ryan know all those people?" Tyler asked me later.

"No, but that's how he'll get to know them," I said. That's just the way he was.

His second year, Ryan joined the Sigma Nu fraternity, moved into the frat house, and really loved the camaraderie. He talked about it all the time; there was something about being part of a community that made him come alive.

His college friends remember him as being very creative and a big kid at heart. He met one of his best friends, Steve Sawalich, early on when they partnered on a project to set up a night of television programming for a fictional TV station. Ryan, Steve, and their other friends loved video games and could often be found playing Bond or NBA Basketball on Nintendo 64. To counteract their couch-potato tendencies, Ryan and Steve started doing Tae Bo, an exercise program that was a mix of martial arts, boxing, and aerobics by a popular fitness instructor named Billy Blanks. Ryan and Steve got hold of Blanks's videotapes and got big into Tae Bo. They were dedicated, got great results, and their enthusiasm was catching. Eventually they started hosting Tae Bo classes at the frat house.

But Steve and Ryan really bonded over their love for film. Ryan's two favorite movies were *Braveheart* and *The Shawshank Redemption*. He liked to watch certain films over and over, and he would memorize the names of all of the actors, no matter how large or small the part. Steve's senior project was a short film starring Ryan called *Saturday Night Loser*. It was a quirky tale about a lovable dorky guy trying to get the attention of a pretty girl.

His senior year at Pepperdine, Ryan was elected president of Sigma Nu. After the election, Ryan became close to a counselor who encouraged him to make the fraternity mean something more than wasting time and partying. So Ryan tried to lead the fraternity in a positive direction—one of his first projects was getting the guys to work together on building houses for Habitat for Humanity.

Not that he was perfect—far from it. Although he was very open with me, I'm sure there's a lot about Ryan and what he's done in his life that he didn't share with me. But we did talk about things I would have thought a son wouldn't talk about with his mother. Maybe our years of my being a single mom drew us extra close. I remember him saying that he was torn about wanting to be a good Christian and waiting to have sex until he was married, but he also knew that his dad and I encouraged our kids not to marry as young as we did. We blamed our marriage problems on our youth, and Ryan and Jessi took that to heart.

"I don't know how long I can wait to have sex," Ryan said. "Should I get married young so I can have sex or wait to get married and maybe not make it to my marriage as a virgin?"

Years later, Ryan opened up to me again. I didn't ask but he told me he hadn't waited. But he had already learned that sex for the physical pleasure alone left him feeling unsatisfied. I don't know any other details of my son's sex life, as I assume most mothers don't, but Ryan also shared with me that when he met a beautiful girl named Kristen at Pepperdine, he thought she might be the one he'd like to spend the rest of his life with. As they grew closer and began to think about the future, they decided to wait until marriage to have sex. I only mention this because this is so unique in our culture. I know that Ryan's heart was to live in a way that honored God, and he was in the process of learning how to put his spiritual life in priority over everything else. That tells you a lot about Ryan.

As his college years drew to a close, Ryan began not only to think about the future but to reflect on his journey, and he wrote his grandparents a letter they still treasure. Here's an excerpt:

Dear Daddy Pat and Mama Shirley,

It has been quite a long time since I wrote you two. I think I might have still been in elementary school the last time I actually put my feelings into words about you both. To be honest, I almost always prefer to communicate face to face, but sometimes taking time to write it down puts a little bit more of an emphasis on the message you are trying to get across. So here it goes.

Obviously, I am going through a vital transitional period in my life right now. The decisions that I make over the next few years are truly pivotal, and will no doubt affect the rest of my life. So many different paths, so many people to choose from to travel the path with. School, fraternities, friends, girls, sports, fitness, volunteerism, jobs, money, and other miscellaneous items to ponder have all snuck up on me over the last few weeks and absorbed all my attention. But every now and then, you get a moment to yourself. And in that moment you take stock of what you have and how you got there . . . and the people who are incredibly special and integral to your life. People like you two.

I think you both know how much I love you and how much I appreciate everything you have done for me. But sometimes just simply saying I love you and thank you isn't enough. I have been thinking about you two a lot lately, and what I have been wanting to do is let you know how blessed I am to have you both in my life. You have had a big part in shaping me into the person I am today, someone who feels loved, able, and ready to take the next step forward towards the rest of my life. You have both let me know, almost relentlessly, that God loves me and has a purpose for me. That you, my grandparents, and my parents love me. And I, even today, still believe that I am a good boy! You instilled these feelings in me and that is the main reason why I wake up every day unafraid and ready to tackle any problems awaiting me. I know that whether I fail or succeed in anything, God is with me, that you all love me, and that I am a good person. I have you two to thank, as well as my parents, for giving me such an at-ease mind and confident spirit.

Something else I want to stress is how much I do wish I could see and talk with you both more. I love spending time with you two, not just because you are my family and I love you, but for the same reason I like to see my friends. I simply enjoy hanging out with you guys. I think that is rare for a grandson to say that about his grandparents, but how many grandparents are as young as you both are and are as fun to be around?

Daddy Pat is clinically insane and I get a kick out of that. Mostly because I am pretty much the same way. And with you, Mama Shirley, all I have to do is get you to start laughing and you won't stop until the following Tuesday. You mix those things in with the fact that you are both extraordinarily intelligent people with strong opinions and that makes for good company.

Lastly, I want to tell you both how proud I am of you. Daddy Pat, you are amazing to me. You are without question one of my most dear role models, along with my dad and Mike. You inspire me to go out and do whatever it is that I want to do no matter what the odds or what the public may say. I have so much respect for you and what you have done with your life. I just hope that I can have your kind of success. That doesn't necessarily mean financial success, but more importantly, the tight family life that you have bred into each and every one of us.

Mama Shirley, I am proud of you as well. You are so important to me. I realize it more and more each day. You gave me my sensitivity and my intense compassion for others. You made me a cuddler, a hugger, and the kind of guy who isn't afraid to say, I love you. You helped mold my heart and you are constantly in it. I love you both so much. Just wanted you to know that.

Love,
Ryan

About this time, we had a family portrait done in Mama and Daddy's backyard in Beverly Hills. The whole family was there—my sisters, their husbands and children, and Mama and Daddy at the center. All of the grandkids naturally grouped around their parents except for Ryan—he stood right next to Daddy Pat. Somehow that special bond forged when Ryan was born and Daddy was just forty-two never weakened. In fact, it seemed to grow stronger. And we would all need to draw on that strength in the days ahead.

CHAPTER 6

"I THINK SOMETHING IS GOING TO HAPPEN TO ME"

*He is just getting himself ready for what's ahead. God's
about to call on him. The wait is just about over.*

FROM RYAN'S SCREENPLAY

As HIS COLLEGE CAREER wound down, Ryan's spirituality
ramped up, and he became very serious about studying the
Bible. He told me about a weekend retreat he'd been to where
he sensed the presence of God. He fell to the ground weeping
and felt the Lord's call to follow him more closely. He had
pretty much settled on being a writer or director and using his
talents as a communicator to share positive, uplifting messages.
His ambition was to make an impact on the world around him
and point others toward Christ.

So Ryan decided to write a screenplay immediately after
graduating from Pepperdine in December 1999. "If I don't
get this down on paper before getting a real job, it might
never get done," I remember him telling his Daddy Pat and
Mama Shirley. He asked them if he could use their house in
Hawaii to hole up for a few months to work on it, and they
agreed. He planned to write a script telling the story of the
Gospel of John set in modern times.

Not long after, Ryan flew to the Islands with his grandparents. They spent ten days together around the Christmas

holidays. Then Mama and Daddy stocked the house with groceries, showered him with hugs and prayers, and left him alone.

As usual, he took some ribbing from his friends. Steve remembers teasing him about "the hard work," figuring that he was studying girls on the beach more than he was working. But for three months Ryan immersed himself in reading and studying the Bible and biblical prophecy to make sure his rendering of the story didn't take too much license as he modernized it. He also read lots of books and watched every movie he could get on the life of Christ.

He seemed to be experiencing a spiritual awakening. Jessi visited him in Hawaii for a week or two and was surprised at Ryan's intensity as he talked about what he'd been learning. One day he said, "Jessi, I think something's going to happen to me." Though he gave no specifics, she never forgot his words.

I had never known him to read a book outside of a class assignment, but he pored over the Scriptures and was an avid reader from that point on, with a passion for the Bible and Bible prophecy. He met God in a more personal way as he pondered the life and ministry of Jesus. He focused on the Gospels, prophecy, and current events, and the Scriptures came alive for him.

His father, Doug, remembers Ryan's fervor. "There was an intensity about him I hadn't seen before. It was almost too much," he said.

Ryan told me he thought the Bible was like a stereogram—designs that were popular in the 1990s. They featured colorful but flat, two-dimensional pictures. If you stared at just the right angle, the three-dimensional images hidden inside began to slowly take shape. Ryan said the Bible is like that—there are images and ideas that run through the whole Bible but you have to spend time looking for and wrestling with them. If you only glance and move on too quickly, you'll miss them.

Ryan came back from Hawaii transformed. Those closest to him could see evidence of heaven's work in his life. He also came back with a finished screenplay called *3:16*, about a very unusual college student in Los Angeles named Yeshua.[11] The story opens in a university lecture hall with a distinguished Jewish scholar in town for a guest lecture. The lecturer begins by asking the student audience of several hundred if anyone can quote Isaiah 61 from memory. A young man named Yeshua stands up and begins to quote: "The Spirit of God is upon me because he has chosen me to speak the good news to the poor. He has sent me to heal the brokenhearted, to tell the prisoners that they will be freed, and to give sight to those who cannot see. To tell the world that the year of God's love has come."

When he is finished, the professor asks Yeshua if he knows who the passage is about. "It's about me," he responds.

"I am sorry but I am not sure if I heard you correctly. Could you repeat that?"

"The prophet was writing about me," Yeshua says. "He was writing about this day."

As you can imagine, there is a tremendous uproar in the auditorium that spreads into the university and, eventually, the city of Los Angeles, as Ryan's story about a modern-day Messiah unfolds, ending with his death and resurrection in the city of Washington, DC. I don't know if the screenplay for *3:16* is good. Some have read it and are very impressed with this as a first attempt. One Hollywood producer even expressed an interest in getting it made. But I do know it changed Ryan's life. It also revealed so much about his understanding of the gospel and his desire to explain the words of Jesus so even new readers of the Bible can understand them.

Not only was Ryan on fire spiritually and talking continually about what he had learned, he had developed a strong interest in biblical prophecy. He believed there were abundant and clear signs that the prophecies pertaining to the last days of human history are set to be fulfilled, and he felt a sense of urgency that he needed to explain these things to those he loved. In his likable, loving way, he decided to sit down with any of his friends who didn't know Jesus Christ to explain the reason for Christ's coming and his death on the cross and resurrection, to the best of his ability. He studied Old Testament prophecy in detail and enjoyed nothing more than explaining how things in one Old Testament book tied into events in another Old Testament book, and then how those events corresponded with the evening news. Ryan felt the clock of history was ticking out its last moments. He didn't want to scare anyone, but he wanted each person he came across to think about who Jesus is and whether he is the Son of God.

Ryan believed time was short.

He kept notes on his computer and welcomed the chance to talk about what he was learning with family and friends. He even met with a couple of the senior pastors at The Church on the Way. They came away impressed, sensing a calling on his life.

One day Ryan called, and after we'd caught up, we began to talk about spiritual things. "Mom, I don't exactly know what it is, but I truly believe God is planning to use me in a big way," Ryan said. "I mean, in a really big way. And I don't think I will be preaching. I think it will be something else. But I don't know what it is."

I felt it too, and told him so. "I feel like King David," he continued. "When he was a shepherd, he had the heart of a king. But when he became a king, he kept the heart of a shepherd. Right now I'm broke and have nothing to offer, but I feel like a king, like God is grooming me for great things. I just have to keep the heart of a shepherd when those things start happening."

Later, I discovered that the name *Ryan* means "kingly." We'd chosen it for no other reason than that we liked the sound of it.

✦ ✦ ✦

As transformative as his Hawaiian experience had been, once he returned home, Ryan's life didn't look any different from that of most recent college grads. He moved into an apartment with his friend Steve. They were joined by a third roommate from Sigma Nu, Grant McGahuey. Their first apartment was in Calabasas, a suburb of Los Angeles in the rugged hills near Malibu Canyon. They found it a long commute to their jobs in the city, so they moved to an apartment on Dorothy Street in Brentwood, a nice neighborhood on the west side of the city that wasn't too far from the beach.

The three guys weren't into the hard-partying Hollywood scene but had no problem keeping themselves entertained.

They still loved video games and once a month held a Video Game Olympics where they would rent five or six games and create a tournament chart to track their scores and determine a winner.

When they weren't playing video games, they watched movies that they took turns picking. The apartment was decorated with their extensive movie poster collection, which they rotated every couple of months. They loved to watch comedies like *A Night at the Roxbury*, starring *Saturday Night Live* stars Will Ferrell and Chris Kattan, over and over. The movie tells the story of two dim-witted and awkward brothers who dream about owning their own nightclub. They also enjoyed movies by the Farrellys, the unconventional movie-making brothers who were just getting started with movies like *Dumb and Dumber*.

Ryan, Steve, and Grant loved to dream about making it in the entertainment industry and sometimes stayed up until three or four in the morning brainstorming ideas and coming up with film and TV projects. Ryan had the idea for a TV show called *The Wannabes*, with three young male characters based on the roommates. One was an actor trying to break into the business, one was an aspiring musician, and one was a quirky guy who kept coming up with wild ideas for getting into the *Guinness Book of World Records*. As he sought his big break, Ryan took a series of odd jobs in retail and restaurants to support himself.

Steve never remembers having even a single fight with Ryan. He describes Ryan as a friend to everyone who made people he'd just met feel as if they'd known him for years. People felt as if they could talk to him about anything.

Besides hanging out with his roommates, Ryan spent a lot of time with Kristen. He felt like she was the one for him, and one foggy day, he took her for a walk at the beach. A flaming tiki torch marked the spot where he'd been earlier and had written, "Kristen, will you marry me?" in the sand. When Kristen saw the message in the sand, she wrote "YES" underneath and they celebrated with champagne. Soon after, they set a wedding date of November 19, 2001.

With marriage and new responsibilities looming, Ryan finally landed a job in "the business." He was hired on as a production assistant at a hugely popular sitcom filmed at CBS Studio Center in the San Fernando Valley, about a half-hour drive from the apartment. It was an exciting opportunity for a young guy who dreamed of creating and writing his own show. Ryan loved working in the writers' bungalow. He fetched coffee, bagels, and dry cleaning, but he also got the chance to observe how the scripts were created and as usual, he made lots of friends among the crew.

One day, however, he was surprised when the head writer called him in for a meeting. Ryan went into his office, nervous and wondering what he'd done wrong.

"Who is your grandfather?"

"Pat Boone," Ryan answered, wondering what was going on.

"Why didn't you tell us? We love Pat Boone! Why don't you bring him over to see us sometime?"

"I didn't think it had anything to do with my work here," said Ryan. He had kept his celebrity roots a secret and was determined to stand on his own two feet and make it without any special favors. Somehow, though, word had gotten out.

✦ ✦ ✦

By this point, Mike and I had been happily married for over a decade. I remembered at times how he had hesitated about moving into marriage when he had a hard time relating to Ryan. I'm so glad I didn't overreact and walk away. Within a few years Mike had watched this skinny, timid, awkward kid stand up and give speeches, win elections, break school basketball records, bungee jump in a thunderstorm, lead his fraternity brothers in college, graduate with a degree in telecommunications, fearlessly pursue a career in the highly competitive entertainment industry, write a screenplay, and fall in love with the Lord. He was special.

And he was relentless. Mike was soon to find out more about that, too.

During our marriage, we had agreed on most things, except for one area—faith. Mike was a strong person and he felt only weak people needed Christ. He never publicly denied the existence of God, but it was his opinion that people needed a God when they felt overwhelmed and that, in good times, nobody turns to God. "I was a coward in that I was afraid to come out and say there was no God," he told me once. But in his heart, Mike felt God and religion were made up by people to serve as a comfort and an emotional defense against the finality and hopelessness of death. "I held on to that for years."

One turning point for Mike came on a cruise to Greece we took for my fortieth birthday back in 1995. One of the cruise stops was in the ancient Greek (and later Roman) city of Ephesus. At one time Ephesus had a population of a quarter of a million people, making it one of the largest cities in the ancient Mediterranean. One of the Seven Wonders of the World was in Ephesus—the Temple of Artemis, goddess of the hunt and associated with fertility. In the old part of the city there is a magnificent marble amphitheater, still mostly intact, that seats 25,000 people. And when we walked off that cruise ship and visited the ancient stadium, something happened to Mike.

"I'll never forget it," Mike said. "We were in the amphitheater listening to the tour guide and I kept wondering, *Who is this Paul they're talking about?*"

Mike asked me who Paul was, and I told him about the Pharisee-turned-Christ-follower who took the Good News outside of the Jewish world and planted churches around the Mediterranean. I was surprised how little Mike knew; to me, this was old news and something I grew up just knowing.

We left the amphitheater and got back on the bus. Within a few minutes, the bus driver pointed out the house where Mary lived. Mike asked, "Mary who?"

"Mary, the mother of Jesus," I answered. According to tradition, Mary was cared for by one of Jesus' best friends, John, who brought her to Ephesus after the Resurrection. The house is called the House of the Virgin, and the building seems to date from the sixth century. However, the foundations are old and it's possible they date back to Mary's time. No one is quite sure. But seeing it had a profound effect on Mike. "It got me past mythology and I began to think about the reality," he said.

When he got home, Mike picked up the Bible and read the book of Ephesians. Then he began to get curious. *I can't say I don't believe in something I haven't read,* he thought. So he read the Bible all the way through, starting in Genesis, chapter 1. Then he read it through again. And again.

"It came into focus," he said. "I started figuring out how it all fit together." When Mike told me that, I remembered how Ryan had compared Scripture to a stereogram. If you give the Bible a cursory read, you will miss what's there. Only when you take the time to look carefully will the complete picture emerge.

Mike and I started to go to Saddleback Church for a weekly Bible study, where my husband continued to look for answers. I was enjoying spending time with my husband and felt God was drawing me closer. But we both always felt awkward when it was time for prayer requests. We felt bad because we never had any! Other people were losing jobs or suffering major illnesses or dealing with chronic pain. Everyone had problems except us. It was absolutely embarrassing and we almost wanted to make something up. I've felt like that for most of my life—like I didn't have any major problems. But just a year or two later, we wouldn't be able to say that anymore. Our turn was coming.

One night, in the middle of a Bible study meeting, a question popped into Mike's mind. He had never considered it before, but something the Bible study leader said made Mike wonder, *Is Jesus God?*

Mike leaned over to me and whispered, "Is he saying that Jesus is God?"

"Yeah, everybody knows that," I whispered back.

Mike was stunned. *How can Jesus be God? Is it that understood?* He was filled with questions and doubts, but he knew there was something there, some truth he didn't quite understand yet with his critical, demanding lawyer's mind. He needed proof, logical evidence that he could put his trust in. He hadn't yet found it, but he wasn't giving up.

And that's where Ryan came in. When Ryan came back from Hawaii with his screenplay on the life of Christ, everyone noticed his passionate interest in prophecy and the Scriptures. You couldn't not notice! Mike was a little concerned. Ryan's enthusiasm reminded him of two high school friends who, right after graduation, decided to follow Jesus and told everyone they were born again. "Nobody had anything to do with them anymore," said Mike. "They got on fire for the Lord and none of us wanted to hear it. They were blocked from our group of friends."

Mike was worried about Ryan and didn't want the same thing to happen to him. So he took him out for dinner, just the two of them.

"I could tell he was on fire for the Lord, and on fire for his interpretation of the Bible, and he wanted to convince everybody," Mike told me. "I wanted him to slow down. I told him blatantly, 'Chill. Cool it! You're going to lose your friends.'"

But privately, Ryan's passion for the Bible and what God was teaching him ignited something in Mike. He was intrigued by Ryan's excitement.

What Mike didn't know was that Ryan had been praying for him daily, that he would come to know Jesus. In addition, Ryan had many discussions with Mike, trying to determine what was preventing his stepdad from coming to faith in Christ. Once Mike raised another objection, Ryan would try to find answers to it. I was so happy to know that Ryan was praying for and talking with Mike. While I adored my husband, I wanted him to know Jesus the way I did.

For a couple of years I, too, had felt drawn to the Lord. I began to long for the close relationship I'd had with God when I was younger. I sensed that God himself was courting me. There were gifts from him that sparked deep adoration, like a video I came across with music from the early years of the Jesus Movement back in the '60s and early '70s. Watching that video triggered deep emotions in me and I could barely get through it without weeping, a cleansing type of quiet sobbing bringing me to repentance and gratitude that he loved me enough to come after me. I knew Mike was searching in earnest and I hoped he would find the answers he needed.

The third time Mike read through the Bible, he started noticing the word *heart*. Mike was a man who operated on intellect. But every time he sat down to read the Bible, he kept reading about a God who cares about more than just brains. "I wanted to understand faith, and every time I read Scripture, it was all about the heart and how much the Lord wants your heart. So I decided to approach the Lord from my heart, because that's where faith comes from. I had been approaching life the wrong way."

It was a long, gradual journey of understanding, but Mike never gave up. On Easter 2001 we attended services at Saddleback Church and Mike picked up a response card and checked box B.

I didn't pay much attention until he showed me the card. Box B said, "I'm placing my hope in Jesus today, trusting him to save me and give me a fresh start and new life."

I looked at him. "I think you checked the wrong box." I thought he hadn't read it carefully.

"No, I checked the right box," he said.

Now *that* was a moment. I was humbled at the goodness and faithfulness of God to pursue me and then my husband. I was a waterfall of tears again.

Mike wanted to tell Ryan personally about his decision, so when he and Kristen came over that day for Easter, I sat quietly and let Mike tell him. Ryan was unbelievably happy and I was reminded again that God answers prayer. I felt we were entering a new era in our marriage and family. Mike felt it too. "I had a new way of approaching life," he said. "I still asked questions, and I always will, but now my heart is there. I'm learning to love the Lord with all of my heart, mind, and soul."

During this time of spiritual searching, Mike decided to slow down the pace of his work. He was tired of the stress and the long hours of his legal practice. Also, he'd taken on a younger partner in the practice who wanted to buy into the business. This partner took much of his day-to-day work-load, relieving the pressure. As a result, Mike was able to cut back his office schedule so that he was in only two days a week. He posted a sign on his desk: *Nobody ever said on their deathbed they wished they'd spent more time in the office.*

Mike took that sentiment to heart and by the time he checked box B on that card at Saddleback, his life was start-ing to look very different from the hectic pace he'd kept when we first met.

I felt as if Mike and I had started a new journey. In fact, the previous fall, when I realized that my two oldest children were taking big steps into adulthood, I had asked Mama and Daddy if we could have a special family dinner around the big maple table. I just wanted to celebrate family, looking back on happy memories and looking forward to a bright future as our two oldest were about to spread their wings and leave the nest for good. We were all there: Mama, Daddy, Doug and his wife, Nana (Doug's mother), Ryan and Kristen, Jessi and her boyfriend, Tyler, Mike, and me. We ate and we laughed and it was a wonderful family time.

After dinner, I put on a song I'd heard for the first time on the radio just a week before: "I Hope You Dance" by Lee Ann Womack. It's one of my favorite songs about not taking life for granted and holding on to the wishes and hopes you have for the ones you love most. And it says that when life gets hard and you're tempted to give up and sit it out, instead rely on faith and *dance*.

It was one of those moments when life slows down, the clock seems to stop, and you're there with your family in a warm, safe bubble of love and joy and expectation and grace. I will never forget that moment. And it was even more special when, as the music played, we got up and danced, two by two, around that big round table. The kids seemed to sense it was a moment I was creating for my mental photo album. Even Tyler, just thirteen, asked Nana, his seventy-nine-year-old grandmother, to dance. Nana's husband had passed away just a month or two before. The experience of all of us dancing in the house I grew up in, to the words of that song, was magical. I'm glad I didn't know then that it would be the last time I would dance with Ryan for a long, long time.

CHAPTER 7

THE VALLEY OF THE
SHADOW OF DEATH

No matter how bad it may look in the coming days . . .
never forget, we win in the end. That's a promise.

FROM RYAN'S SCREENPLAY

WHEN RYAN CRASHED down through the skylight, Steve's first impulse had been to reach out and grab him. But Steve couldn't; it happened too fast. He stood there for a second, in shock. Then he wheeled around and darted back through the access door.

As he ran down the stairs from the roof he thought, *I'll find him on the third floor walkway.* He'd help Ryan up, they'd go down to the apartment and ice his bumps and bruises, and maybe have a good laugh about it later. Worst case scenario, he'd have a broken leg or ankle.

But Ryan wasn't on the third floor.

Steve looked over the wall bordering the walkway and saw Ryan. He was on the bottom floor lying on his right side, legs splayed out, and he wasn't moving. He was still wearing his backpack.

Steve ran down the stairs to the bottom and over to Ryan. He was unconscious, a star-shaped spray of blood under his head, and his breathing sounded rough, almost like he was

87

gasping for air. He'd fallen almost forty feet to a concrete floor. But he was alive. It was 3:50 p.m.

Two men who'd been working on an apartment across the courtyard came running to try to help. No one had cell phones on them, so as soon as Steve knew Ryan wouldn't be alone, he sprinted back up the stairs to the apartment. He burst in the front door and yelled at Grant, still playing video games. "Call 911! Ryan fell!" As soon as Grant punched in the number, Steve grabbed the cordless phone to talk to the 911 operator.

As he started answering the operator's questions, he walked quickly back out the front door and over to the wall so he could look over the top and see Ryan down below. Grant ran down the stairs to get to Ryan but Steve stayed put; he was afraid that he'd lose reception on the cordless phone if he got too far away from the apartment and went out of range. Steve remembers telling the operator about Ryan's breathing—by this point it was rougher and Steve told her it sounded like Ryan was snoring. He could hear it clearly from up on the second floor walkway.

Steve waited on the phone with the emergency operator but got frustrated. She seemed to be trying to keep him calm, asking him strange questions like "Isn't it a nice day out?" That question was the only thing he remembers the operator saying because it was so odd. His heart was pounding and he wanted to get back downstairs to be with Ryan.

The paramedics finally arrived. It felt like hours but it had been just four minutes since Steve had called. As soon as they arrived, he hung up and ran downstairs to join Grant as the paramedics and firefighters bustled around Ryan. The first responders did a quick assessment, then gave him oxygen, started an IV, and put him on an EKG monitor. The two roommates stood back and watched, wanting to help but knowing they couldn't. The atmosphere was grim; the only sounds were the businesslike comments as the paramedics focused on stabilizing Ryan, and above it all, the awful sound of his ragged breathing.

Someone came over to Steve and Grant and said, "Call his family because it doesn't look good." Just after that, the paramedics packed him up and loaded Ryan into the ambulance out front.

Steve and Grant ran to Steve's car to follow the ambulance to UCLA Medical Center. On the way, Grant called Shirley on his cell phone. They both knew Mike, Tyler, and I were in Spain, and they didn't know how to reach us, so they figured calling Mama Shirley was the next best thing.

"Ryan's been in an accident," Steve told Mama. "He had a fall and they're taking him to UCLA. You need to come down there."

As soon as the guys arrived at the hospital, they called Ryan's fiancée, Kristen. She worked at a bank in Orange County. She was in the vault, they were told. "Can you call back later?"

"No, you need to pull her out of the vault," Steve said. When Kristen answered the phone and heard what happened, she began crying hysterically. Steve underplayed the seriousness of the situation. He knew she had to navigate rush hour traffic and might have an hour's drive ahead of her. They planned to fill her in on the details once she arrived at the hospital.

Ryan was wheeled into the emergency room at 4:12 p.m., just over twenty minutes after the fall. Not only was he unconscious and unresponsive, but he had massive head trauma along with a large abrasion over the left side of his ribs. His skin was pale, cool, and moist. The pupil of his left eye was fixed and dilated. The records show that back at 4:05 p.m., when Ryan was first loaded into the ambulance, paramedics had been unable to obtain a blood pressure reading—his EKG had flatlined. Because of the tremendous impact, Ryan was bleeding internally and he'd gone into shock.

Paramedics assessed him as a 3 on the Glasgow Coma Scale (the highest score for a healthy conscious person is 15). Ryan was at the lowest level of consciousness possible without actually dying. But somehow he was still breathing, however weak and rattled it was.

The ER staff had their hands full as they tackled multiple problems to try to keep Ryan alive. He had multiple fractures to the right side of his skull and his face, along with multiple contusions. His brain was swelling from the terrific impact, resulting in dangerous pressure. His jaw was broken in four places. His neck was not broken, but he had swelling in the spinal area from the impact. His lungs were severely bruised and punctured. He had trauma to his heart, and blood was leaking into his chest. He had multiple rib fractures. His spleen basically exploded from the impact, shooting blood throughout his abdominal cavity. His liver was lacerated and bleeding. He had some fractures in his pelvic bones. The internal injuries filled his lungs with blood. His body was in shock and had suffered so much damage that it was barely functioning. Because of the structural damage, his internal organs weren't working well, and he quickly went into severe metabolic acidosis, a very destructive chemical imbalance in his blood that needed to be reversed quickly. Emergency blood work also showed coagulopathy, which meant his blood was not clotting properly.

Nurses, doctors, and technicians surrounded him during those first few crucial moments, checking his vitals, hooking him up to large-bore IVs, and drawing blood for tests. Through it all, Ryan felt nothing. He was completely unconscious as the activity swirled around him.

Ryan's injuries were mostly upper body and seemed to be mainly on the right side. No one saw the actual fall after he broke through the fiberglass, but we learned later that when people fall any significant distance, they typically fall on their heads. In most people the upper body is heavier than the lower half of the body and so, in a fall, "the person tips over and plunges head-downward, like an arrow with a weighted point."[12] In *The Wild Trees*, a book about scientists searching for (and climbing, and sometimes falling out of) the world's largest trees, Richard Preston explains that an adult can easily die even in a ten-foot fall if he happens to land on his head. One tree-climbing expert was giving a safety demonstration, made an error, and fell just fifteen feet. He broke his neck and died right in front of his students.[13]

Fifty-foot falls are almost always fatal, with a headfirst landing resulting in a crushed skull, broken neck, and internal organs hemorrhaging from the impact. If the body cavity fills with blood and the bleeding can't be stopped, the result can be catastrophic internal hemorrhage. The body bleeds out, and after a bit, the body just stops working. Or the lungs fill up with blood and the person drowns.

Ryan's fall was between thirty and forty feet, and the main impact points seemed to be the right side of his head and face, his chest and right side, and his hips. Later, when my husband, Mike, went to take a look at the accident site, he noticed a freshly indented oval-shaped area in the top of the concrete wall on the second floor walkway, directly under the broken skylight. He also saw what looked like damage to the third floor wall. When Ryan broke through, his body most likely began to rotate and turn upside down. He hit the third floor walkway wall on the way down and bounced off, then hit the second floor wall. The force of the impact on the second floor wall created the indent, removed some paint, and caused a crack along the edge of the concrete. It's likely the indent was caused by his head, fracturing his skull and jaw. He bounced off the second floor wall, then fell the rest of the way to the first floor. His injuries showed that he probably landed at an angle that distributed the impact equally across the right side of his head and upper body. And although he hit two walls on the way down, it may very well be that the walls broke his fall, slowed him down, and kept him from falling a full thirty feet and landing directly on his head and neck. It also may be that hitting the two walls knocked him unconscious, and he may not have even felt the final impact when he hit the ground.

Although he was alive, much of his upper body, including his head, was broken and battered, and Ryan was in grave danger. At 4:15 p.m., records show his blood pressure and oxygen ratings began to drop. Nurses pushed blood and fluids into him through the IVs. His numbers would go up, then drop again. At 5:00 p.m., he was rushed into surgery. The internal bleeding had to be stopped, or he wouldn't make it.

At this point, no one had been allowed in to see him.

As soon as Mama got the call from Steve and Grant, she dropped everything and rushed to the hospital with Marina, her housekeeper. But Daddy assumed it was probably something like a broken arm, and my mother could handle it without him. I think mothers are wired to consider that an accident is serious until proven otherwise and men are the reverse—it's not serious until proven otherwise.

Mama and Marina prayed hard during the five-minute drive, sensing that it was going to be bad. Marina dropped Mama off at the entrance to the emergency room. As she approached the glass doors, some paramedics came out of a door nearby. Mama could hear them talking about a bad fall and so she went up to one of them and said, "That was my grandson. How is he?"

"Lady, don't get your hopes up," he said.

Once doctors told her how serious Ryan's injuries were, she called Daddy at his office. Then she sat down near Steve and prayed while she waited. Daddy arrived a few minutes later, and Mama told him what little she knew.

Steve was in shock, trying hard not to think about what he had just seen on the rooftop. "When Pat got there, he led us in prayer. When he started praying Psalm 23, with 'Yea, though I walk through the valley of the shadow of death,' Grant and I opened our eyes and looked at each other. It was becoming real."

The small group huddled together, waiting for a report from the doctors. When the news came an hour or so later, it was all bad. The doctors said Ryan's lungs had collapsed from the impact and they didn't know how long he had gone without sufficient oxygen. His spleen had burst; they had removed it in surgery, but he was still bleeding internally. His skull was fractured, his jaw and ribs were broken, and they suspected a spinal cord injury in the cervical column.

"People in Ryan's condition don't usually make it," they said.

As my mother tells it, although she heard the words of the paramedic and then later the doctors, she felt no fear. She just focused on an even louder voice coming from within: *He will live and not die and declare the glory of God.*

I remember how Mama had showed me her strength during another crisis back when Ryan and Jessi were just four and three. I needed to run an errand, so I left Jessi with Mama at my parents' house. I walked outside, got into the station wagon, started the engine, and began backing down the driveway. What I didn't know was that Jessi had come outside to say good-bye. We figured out later she must have darted out the side door. I never saw her, but as I reversed the car and rolled backward I felt a bump, then heard loud screams. I hit the brakes and had no idea what was going on. *Was that Jessi? Oh no. I think I just hit her!*

I jumped out of the car to try to get to the sound of the screaming but in my panic, I neglected to throw the car into park. As I jumped out, the car started rolling backward. Time went into slow motion and I couldn't understand what was happening. I froze, somehow knowing the car was rolling over her but there wasn't anything I could do to stop it. The car rolled a few feet, hit a curb, then stopped against a tree. I ran and then found myself standing next to the car, frozen. Jessi was up, crying and screaming at the top of her lungs, so I knew she was still alive. There was blood on her face and leg.

Mama heard Jessi's shrieks, ran outside, scooped her up, and hurried back into the house. I finally made myself walk inside. I was terrified at what I would see. I was so afraid of what had happened that I didn't want to look. I couldn't look.

That's a very hard thing for a mother to say, but it's the truth. I could not look.

But that time it was all okay. Jessi was sitting on her Mama Shirley's lap, crying, but okay. "Let's get her to the doctor," Mama said.

On the way to the doctor's office, Jessi continued to wail, "Mommy, Mommy—why'd you put the wheels on me, Mommy?" She checked out with some bumps and bruises, but no broken bones. She had tire marks on her leg and arm and it was clear the station wagon had rolled over her but she was so young that her bones were flexible and could still bend instead of break. It could have been so much worse but it wasn't; Jessi was going to be fine. And I was grateful for a mother who could fill in the gaps. She had spent so much time with Ryan and Jessi that she loved them as if they were her own children. She has the ability to stay calm in a crisis. And her faith is so near the surface, I almost think of her as a different kind of first responder, sent by God to meet a crisis head-on with a brave heart and a spirit fueled by faith.

So while Mike, Tyler, and I were still asleep in the vacation condo in Spain, my parents sat in the waiting room and prayed and resisted fear. Family and friends began to fill up the waiting room, and the search to find my phone number in Spain began. We hadn't anticipated any trouble and hadn't thought to arrange for international cell service. The relatives who were staying at our house while we were gone didn't answer the phone at first, and they were the only ones who had our number. Finally, several hours later, someone got the number from them and Debby called me to give me the news.

"Lindy, we've been trying to reach you. Nobody knew the number where you were staying. It's Ryan. He's had an accident."

This time, it didn't matter if I couldn't look. I was too far away.

While we traveled across the world to get back to California, Ryan received thirty-six units of blood as the medical team struggled to keep him alive long enough for us to see him. In a strange coincidence, my dad had been at UCLA Medical Center just a couple of days before for a blood drive with some of his Hollywood chums like Charlton Heston and Shirley Jones. Did Ryan get some of his Daddy Pat's blood? I wonder.

Doug told me later that once Ryan was out of the ER and in intensive care, the nurses waived the rules for strict visiting hours and let anyone and everyone in to see him. They didn't expect Ryan to make it so they were letting family and friends in for a final good-bye. I'm glad I didn't know about that at the time. I'm also glad I didn't know that Ryan's heart had stopped two different times during the heroic efforts to save his life. All this while I slept in Spain.

Mike had a shock when we changed planes in Florida after crossing the Atlantic. His cell phone finally worked again and he started listening to voice mail. There was a message from

Ryan. "I'm calling to wish you a Happy Father's Day," he said, "and to tell you what a great stepfather you are." Ryan's voice was warm as ever and Mike could barely take it in. His eyes filled with tears.

Mike played the voice mail for me. I bawled and drank in Ryan's voice, listening hard to every word. It soothed and cut me at the same time.

Hearing the recording made Mike think of how Ryan had dropped us off at the airport when we left for Spain. He got up early so we didn't have to worry about catching a shuttle. Mike kept telling him to drive faster. Ryan fired back and they had a good time teasing back and forth. We didn't know that would be our last interaction with Ryan for a very long time.

During the flight home, Mike kept thinking about a book he'd read in college called *Johnny Got His Gun*, about a young soldier who suffers a horrific war injury and ends up with no arms or legs, a prisoner in a body that no longer works. He hoped Ryan wouldn't end up like that.

Tyler didn't cry or say much on the journey home. We had a little more information each time we talked to Debby, but although we didn't have the whole picture yet, somehow I knew Ryan was in a life-and-death struggle. I chose to believe that heaven heard and that Ryan would be restored to us. Where else could I put my hope?

When we finally arrived at Los Angeles International Airport after a twenty-four-hour journey, my sister Debby was there to pick us up and take us directly to UCLA Medical Center. She was calm, and I was relieved to have her with me. When we arrived I wanted to get to Ryan so badly, yet I was surprised to find how hard it was to make my legs carry me from the waiting area through the double doors and around the corner to the left to his hospital bed. I had to force myself to put one foot in front of the other. There's just no way to prepare yourself for the awful sight of a child of yours, even if he is six-four and twenty-four years old, not moving and hooked up to every imaginable type of machine.

I was afraid, but I looked.

Ryan's face and body were swollen. He was totally unconscious, nothing moving, with tubes in his chest, in his head, and down his throat. His right eye was bloody and puffy and his face was twice its normal size. It was very hard to be in that room. I wanted to be there for him but I couldn't spend much time there. It was a relief to step back into the seventh-floor ICU waiting room where I could talk to the family about all of the details of the last twenty-four hours. It was a great comfort to be surrounded by Mike, Mama, Daddy, Jessi, Tyler, Debby, Doug, and his wife, Vic. Ryan's roommates were there too.

Jessi had come down from San Francisco as soon as she'd received the call from her dad telling her about Ryan's accident. When we had a quiet moment alone in the waiting room, she handed me a journal. On the first page, she had written this:

Mom, this journal is your release . . . use it to express everything and anything. If there was ever a time to rise to an occasion and be courageous—it's NOW. We all need to be positive and hope filled, not only for Ryan but for each other.

I love you,
Jessi

The little girl who had survived that run-in with the station wagon so many years before was now a woman of courage and wisdom. And that journal, passed from daughter to mother, became one of my lifelines. Thank you, Jessi. Here is my everything and anything.

CHAPTER 8

MIDNIGHT IS ONLY SIXTY SECONDS LONG

You told me from the beginning that this day would come.
You told me that he had a much bigger purpose than anything
I could imagine. But still, I'm afraid.

FROM RYAN'S SCREENPLAY

THE FIRST NIGHT was a precarious one for Ryan. His blood pressure kept dropping, along with his oxygen levels. The two-hour emergency surgery had repaired some of the internal damage, but the medical team had to aggressively pump IV fluids and blood into him to keep him alive. Medical notes reported his condition during surgery as "extremely unstable."

Once Ryan arrived in the ICU, records show that his heart rate and blood pressure dropped again and he had problems breathing. The medical team wanted to transport him to another floor for a CAT scan. To do so, they had to remove him from the ventilator and use a breathing bag to push oxygen directly into his lungs. But they quickly realized that his lungs were too damaged from both the trauma and the continued bleeding to transport him safely. The CAT scan had to be postponed. Mama heard whispers that at one point his heart had stopped. His records stated flatly, "Prognosis considered poor."

The details of those next few days are a blur. But I do remember this: the waiting room was filled with Boone family and friends. My sister Cherry flew down from Seattle with her daughter Brittany for a few days. My sister Debby, who lived nearby, was a constant presence. Ryan's roommates and fraternity brothers were often there. Kristen was there. Doug and Vic were there. Mike, Jessi, and Tyler were almost always there. (Tyler was still on summer vacation. Ryan's roommates and Doug made a point of hanging out with Tyler in those early days, taking him to lunch or outside to throw a football around.) I have a precious picture of Mike and Tyler in the waiting room, heads together, sitting up but sound asleep. Daddy was there often, always an energetic and positive presence. And Mama? She was there with me every day, all day.

One thing that hit me during those early weeks at UCLA is that what we were experiencing—the waiting and watching and praying and crying in hospital waiting rooms—goes on all the time. Of course, we weren't the only ones there, and I began to think about all the carefree days I'd spent following my routine, stressing over the small stuff, and never even noticing the many hospitals I drove by or thinking about the hearts breaking at any given moment inside their walls.

Those waiting rooms at UCLA Medical Center were full before our family took up residence there. They filled again after we left. And they are full today. Until your life brings you to one of these seasons of grief and waiting, you never really think about it. But now I do and it has changed me.

I also gained new appreciation for the doctors, nurses, and other professionals who, day after day, find a way to do their jobs, be efficient, show empathy, and yet detach themselves enough so they are not overcome by the inevitable sadness of the circumstances they encounter.

As Ryan lay in his room in the ICU, full of tubes, wrapped in bandages, lifeless, I could hardly bear to look at him. He was so damaged, and I felt helpless and so frightened of the unknown—what he was experiencing, what the future might hold, all of it. I needed to be with him but could hardly bear the pain of it. I could only stand it in small doses.

I didn't want it to be real.

After I got back from Spain, I spent the first nights sleeping in the waiting room. Then Mike and I started sleeping at my parents' house, five minutes away, but I was at the hospital almost every waking moment. Just a couple of days after the accident, I woke up one morning and felt the anxiety start to build as it did every morning. I looked at my watch and it was 5:22 a.m. I had been praying and crying and pleading for God to come and heal Ryan. I pictured my son opening his eyes, sitting up, raising that left eyebrow like he always did, and saying, "Hi, Mom!" with a big warm smile on his face. But it hadn't happened.

Now my prayer changed and I cried out to God, "Teach me. Talk to me."

What came to mind was the story of Lazarus, one of Jesus' best friends, who died young. All of Lazarus's family and friends felt exactly the way I did, the way all of us did. We knew the power of Jesus, and we wanted him to use it for Ryan *now*.

But when Jesus first heard about his friend's illness, he didn't act quickly. He stayed where he was. When Jesus finally traveled to Bethany, Lazarus's hometown, his friend had already died. Lazarus's sisters, Mary and Martha, were grief stricken. The whole town was mourning.

Jesus knew Lazarus was dead, but he also knew something

else: "Lazarus's sickness will not end in death," he had told his disciples before they'd left for Bethany. "No, it happened for the glory of God" (John 11:4). To Jesus, waking Lazarus from the dead was no different than waking him from sleep.

I wrote this in my journal:

What frightens me can't frighten God because his perspective is so different from mine. He sees the story from beginning to end and has the power to write the story. It is as if I could use this pen to write the ending of this story just the way I want it to come out. I could get creative and think of dramatic situations to influence the characters in this story but I don't have the power or the skill. God does.

When Jesus finally arrived at the tomb of his friend, Martha said through her tears, "I know that even now you could bring him back to life."

"Your brother will come back to life again," Jesus said.

"Yes, when everyone else does on Resurrection Day," Martha replied.[14] She didn't understand that Jesus meant "today." I relate to Martha and I found myself wondering if God would do what I knew he could do. And it comforts me that even though Martha doubted, her doubt didn't stop Jesus from doing what he had come there to do—awaken Lazarus.

I added this in my journal:

That comforts me when I worry that if my faith isn't strong enough, the miracle I long for won't happen.

When Jesus arrived at the tomb of his friend, he prayed, "Father, thank you for hearing me. You always hear me, but I said it out loud for the sake of all these people standing here, so that they will believe you sent me" (John 11:41-42). Jesus was modeling for us what to do when we pray. He could have prayed privately, but this was a miracle intended for a purpose—to bring glory to God. People had to hear Jesus call on God so that God would get the glory from the miracle.

I didn't know that something similar was about to happen to me and to Ryan on international television.

As I headed downstairs and got ready to go back to the hospital after that moment with the Lord, I began to weep. The pain I felt down to the core of my being was so strong it felt physical, tangible. I had been reading the story of Lazarus, and I'd seen the parallels to what was happening to Ryan. I'd cried. I'd prayed.

And then something strange happened. I felt it in my spirit, as if I were overhearing a conversation between the Lord and Ryan's spirit in some private spiritual realm.

Ryan.

Yes, Lord.

Do you trust me?

Completely.

Do you want to be used to bring glory to my name?

Oh, yes. I want to be used. Use me.

Do you want your life to count for what matters most? To glorify God and point others toward Christ?

More than anything else, Lord. You know I want that.

Ryan.

Yes, Lord.

Do you trust me?
Completely.

I pondered that moment in my heart that morning as I headed off to the hospital for the day. There wasn't much change in Ryan at this point. He was still barely hanging on; people were going in and out of his room to see him, and the waiting room was always full. We talked, cried, laughed, sang, and prayed. Ryan's dad said we turned the waiting room into a church.

That night, as I prepared to sleep in the hospital waiting room, I put on a CD that Maria, my mother's dear friend and prayer partner, had given me. Maria is one of God's prayer warriors, and she walked the hospital corridors, talking to God constantly in a whisper or laying hands on the door to the ICU as she prayed. She is a tiny woman, a professional dancer who appeared in *West Side Story.* She married one of Daddy's friends and has been Mama's best friend for many years. Maria's quiet, calm energy always made me feel better. So when she gave me something to listen to, I paid attention.

On this night I waited until everyone else was gone so I could focus on the recorded message. After lying down on the floor in a pile of blankets, I put in my earphones and turned on the CD. I listened to the booming voice of an African American preacher, who was giving a message he called "Midnight." He told the story of Paul and Silas, two early missionaries who were in jail, in chains, and "about midnight [they] were praying and singing" (Acts 16:25, ESV). Not only were they praising God in their circumstances, but they did it in the darkest hour, at midnight.

The preacher said midnight is the deepest time of night,

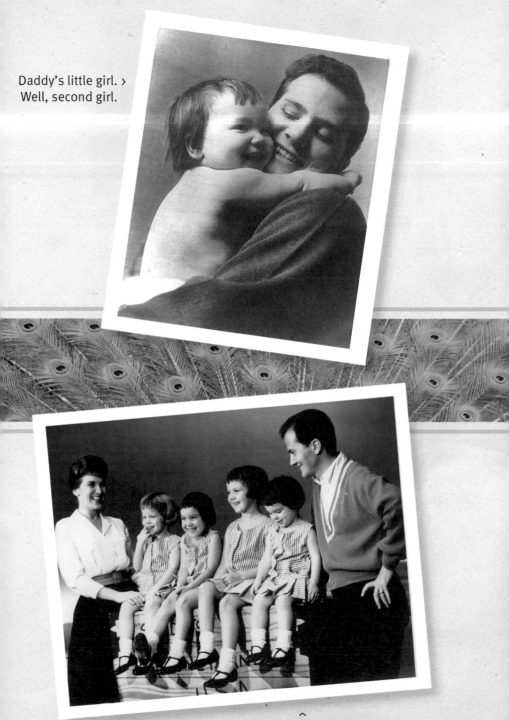

Daddy's little girl. ›
Well, second girl.

The big send-off on Daddy's TV show in New
York before moving the family to California.

The biggest ham is the second Boone girl from the left. Can you tell I loved performing?

^ Proud parents looking on as my sisters and I sing. Nothing's really changed.

‹ Four daughters
in 3 ½ years and
all teenagers at
the same time!

Singing together ›
kept us close and that
closeness remains to
this day.

*Clockwise from
upper left:*
Daddy (Pat), me,
Debby, Cherry,
Mama (Shirley),
and Laury.

Ryan at 4 years old. I still melt at that sweet face. ⌄

Me with Ryan all grown up. ›

^ Ryan's baptism by his Daddy Pat in the backyard pool when he was 12 years old.

No words can describe the feeling of seeing one you love in this kind of condition. ⌄

Ryan had lost 50 pounds,
still needed a respirator, and could not
connect with us at all here.

While Ryan still lies in a coma, his dad, Doug, lovingly gives him a shave. ⌄

^
Joy of all joys! This is the first kiss I got from Ryan after nearly 4 months in the hospital!

Seven months after the accident Larry King visits
Ryan at his care facility where he is still unable to
talk but not considered in a coma.

MIRACLE BY PRAYER?
▶ PAT BOONE'S GRANDSON OUT
OF COMA FROM FREAK FALL

THREESIXT

Mike wasn't sure he would be a good
stepdad to Ryan—how wrong he was!

One of Ryan's first smiles when we had a camera to catch it before it faded.

Far from being in a vegetative state, Ryan lives, loves, and joins in our family fun.

the darkest hour, the most lonely moment of the day or night, but midnight is only sixty seconds long. And God is looking for people to praise him at midnight. So I praised him. And I remembered to keep thanking God that our midnight was temporary. Midnight would end.

I fell asleep listening to the preacher talk and woke up the next morning at exactly 5:22 a.m. again. God spoke to my heart, saying, *It's time for our appointment.* I listened to more of the message from the night before, then I sat up and looked at a picture of Ryan and Kristen. I smiled and remembered telling the hospital chaplain that it made me feel good to talk about Ryan so that others would know what a gentle soul he is. As that thought crossed my mind, I heard the Lord whisper, *I want you to feel good talking about Jesus to others. You ought to want others to understand about the Jesus you know.*

I wrote in my journal:

God is doing something here. Every life that touches this situation is being transformed. We won't ever be the same. What Satan meant for ill, God will use for good. It's begun. We aren't alone. I feel his presence. He is in complete control. God is doing something big here.

Throughout that first week, Ryan continued to be in a coma. His blood was not coagulating, he was on maximum ventilator support, and he was completely unresponsive. But even though I was afraid, grief stricken, and in shock, deep down I did not think he was going to die. I'd believed for a long time, along with Ryan, that God was going to use him somehow to reach out and bring people to himself.

I sensed something going on beneath the surface. Plans were underway. And I was ready for whatever God had in mind.

One week after the accident, early in the morning, the phone in the waiting room rang loudly and startled everyone. I'd been sleeping on the floor in a tangle of blankets. A young girl got up and answered it. It was a wrong number. In a sleepy voice, Mike said, "Hi, honey. It's 5:22 a.m." Was that God's wake-up call again? I rolled over and waited but didn't feel anything from the Lord. Why the call?

I got up and went to see Ryan. The nurse said his night was uneventful, which is always good news in the ICU. I said, "Good morning, Ryan," in my cheeriest voice and then it happened—his eye twitched. I kept talking to him and saw it again, the first muscle movement I'd seen so far. It was so small, but so significant. I felt stronger and said, "Ryan, this is the day. You always want to please. You've always willingly done anything I've asked you to do."

The need of the moment was for Ryan's breathing to stabilize and get stronger so he could get off the ventilator long enough to have a CAT scan on his brain.

"I'm asking you to make this the day, Ryan." My voice was getting stronger, my words clearer. "Fight, breathe, tell Jesus this is the day you want to start your journey back. Do this, Ryan. It would please me so much." His eye twitched several times. I wasn't quite sure what to think of it.

I went back to the waiting room where everyone was still asleep and curled up in the blankets on the floor. I woke up again at 7:45 with an urgent thought: *Read the story of Joshua and the battle of Jericho.* I fumbled for my Bible, and Mike handed it to me. I tried to look it up but my eyes weren't that good with small print anymore. Finally Mike found it and read to me from Joshua 6:

> The LORD said to Joshua, "I have given you Jericho, its king, and all its strong warriors. You and your fighting men should march around the town once a day for six days. . . . On the seventh day you are to march around the town seven times, with the priests blowing the horns. When you hear the priests give one long blast on the rams' horns, have all the people shout as loud as they can. Then the walls of the town will collapse, and the people can charge straight into the town." . . .
>
> When the people heard the sound of the rams' horns, they shouted as loud as they could. Suddenly, the walls of Jericho collapsed, and the Israelites charged straight into the town and captured it.
> (vv. 2-5, 20)

I wrote in my journal:

This is the seventh day. This passage impressed upon me the importance of believing in victory even when it seems like it's crazy to do so. The conventional way to victory would have been a much different military strategy. But God wanted it to be obviously his work. How ridiculous those instructions were, but his people obeyed and the walls came crumbling down.

Bring the walls down today, Lord. Show us how to pray, and we will obey.

Later that morning I went running. My body needed the run, but my spirit needed it even more. I chose the route I've run so many times in my life—directly out the driveway of my parents' house and then left at the end of the block. I ran on the old cracked sidewalks where roots tried to break up and out of the concrete. I ran past the beautiful mansions of Beverly Hills with their palm tree sentinels. It felt good to be out in the fresh air. When I got to Benedict Canyon, I waited for the traffic to break so I could get across to Roxbury.

I waited. And I waited. I walked up the street to see if I could find a place where it would be easier to cross. I was getting frustrated. *How am I going to continue my run if I can't cross this barrier?* And of course I thought of Ryan. His barrier at the moment was breathing on his own.

All of a sudden, I saw a break in the traffic, and I felt a burst of energy flow through me. I cried out to Ryan's spirit, "This is it. Let's go! Come on," as I darted through the cars to the other side. I felt like I was running with Ryan, and I had to encourage him to keep going.

"Come on, Ryan. I'm with you, Ryan. Don't stop, Ryan."

"Breathe!"

I started to push my own lungs to work harder and picked up the pace. As words came to my mind, I spoke them aloud.

"Breathe . . . Strong . . . Healthy . . . Healed . . . Lungs." Then again. "Breathe . . . Strong . . . Healthy . . . Healed . . . Lungs!" Over and over on every fourth step, I spoke a word.

Then I felt I needed to push harder and work for Ryan, to be strong for and with my son. I got louder and louder. I remembered that the Israelites shouted on the seventh day and that was all God required after they finished circling the city. We do the easy part. God does the hard, the impossible part. So I began to shout.

"Breathe! Strong! Healthy! Healed! Lungs! Jesus! Jesus! Now, Jesus. Thank you, Jesus. Hallelujah, Jesus.

"Come on, Ryan. Stay with me. Come on, Ryan, come back. Be healed. I'm here. I'm with you. He's with you. Do it now.

"Breathe . . . Strong . . . Healthy . . . Healed . . . Lungs!"

I ran and shouted all the way down Sunset Boulevard, feeling as if the Holy Spirit had shown me how to pray to bring down the walls and get Ryan across his barrier. Back at my parents' house, housekeepers Marina and Vilma were in the kitchen and remarked on how sweaty I was. I had to circle the kitchen awhile to get my heart rate to come down, and as I started to tell them about my experience, it began all over again. "Breathe . . . Strong . . . Healthy . . . Healed . . . Lungs!" Vilma, Marina, and I shouted to the Lord as I circled the table. I will never forget that moment.

Later that day doctors did a few simple tests on Ryan. They touched his cornea and he blinked. They ran a pen up the sole of his foot and his toes curled in. "Good signs," they said. We were happy.

Mama rubbed Ryan's feet with lotion. Daddy rubbed Ryan's hands and prayed. Debby came in and sang "With Every Breath That I Take," about praising the Lord with all of the strength in your heart. I took a turn rubbing Ryan's feet while I harmonized with my sister, adoring Jesus, cherishing Ryan.

The next morning I read something that renewed my

hope for the day: "Healing is not a result of what we do. It is a result of what Christ has *already done*."[15]

Ryan would finally get a CAT scan a few days later.

✦ ✦ ✦

About a week after the accident, we had a meeting with the doctors. Dr. Paul Vespa, Ryan's neurologist, along with some nurses and a social worker, joined me, Mike, Doug, and Daddy in the conference room. Even Tyler came, although we had told him he could wait and hear the news later.

I had to force myself to walk into the conference room. That morning I'd been listening to another CD from Maria's church, a message called "From Breakdown to Breakthrough." The voice on the CD began to talk about discouragement, but I didn't make it to the breakthrough part before it was time to meet. There were whispers that the news was going to be "not so encouraging." But I knew I had to face whatever the doctor said. I couldn't run away.

I sat stoically as Ryan's neurologist explained the problems with his lungs and the swelling in his brain. Depending on the CAT scan results, Dr. Vespa anticipated a series of operations, including an insertion of a feeding tube to the stomach and probably a tracheotomy, too. His next comments started me down into a scary, dark place. He said there was considerable doubt about whether there would ever be any significant recovery of Ryan's brain function. He even suggested Ryan might have to be kept on a ventilator permanently, which meant he would never come home. I don't remember his exact words, but the doctor asked how we felt about continuing to treat Ryan so aggressively with what was most likely going to be a grim outcome. I felt numb and didn't know what to say. It seemed so hopeless.

Daddy asked some questions about Ryan's brain damage. They explained that for the first twelve hours, Ryan's internal bleeding was so severe that they felt his brain was oxygen deprived, causing extensive damage. I think I lost touch for a few moments; I wanted to tune out the questions and explanations because the more I understood, I realized the less hope they were giving us. I knew the Lord had prepared me for discouragement, but that didn't make me feel it less. Yet for the moment I had an unexpected calm and control over my tears.

We told the team we appreciated them so much and knew it must be hard to have to tell families such difficult news. Then Daddy asked the medical team to keep on doing everything humanly possible for Ryan. He told them we understood the doctor's projections about Ryan's outcome, but we had a better prognosis in mind for Ryan. "We'll take Ryan in whatever state he ends up in," Daddy said, "but we know a God who has intervened in other situations against all odds, and we believe he will again, for Ryan."

Then Doug spoke up. "The way I see it, we have two teams here. You are the medical team, working on Ryan's physical body. And we're the spiritual team, ministering to his spirit." His voice was calm and strong. "Combined, we believe Ryan can get well."

Soon after, Dr. Vespa left the meeting while the other staff remained behind. The social worker remarked that they have many meetings like this with families but rarely does a family try to comfort the staff. Two of the nurses told us that the staff had noticed the uniqueness of our family and how we treated each other. As we left, I felt the medical team was encouraging us to keep up what we were doing and not to let go of our hope.

But I'd had enough. The bad news about Ryan's future was starting to sink in. I realized he was not going to just wake up and step back into his old life. His job, his dreams for the future, his November wedding to Kristen—all of those things were gone. At this point, according to the doctors he might never even get out of the hospital. I hurried to the restroom where I could weep in private.

Two older women walked in and saw my tears. One held me and let me sob. I told her in a few words that we'd had a hard report from the doctor. She said, "But who is the Great Physician?"

"The Lord," I answered.

After the women left, I called out to the Lord to calm and comfort me. Then I took a walk in the gardens outside, came back in to the waiting room to lie down, and escaped into sleep.

Looking back, I realize I was still numb and in shock in those early days. Once I saw Ryan's broken body, I had to spend days and weeks getting to the place where I could draw a line in the sand and determine to stand in faith rather than sink in despair. I learned that perseverance is developed; it's not automatic.

I hadn't been sleeping long when a gastroenterologist came in from checking on Ryan. He looked a little lighter and happier than usual. We gathered together to listen.

"There is some movement in Ryan's legs, arm, and head," he said.

I was cautious, but hopeful. *This has to be good, right?*

"I'm not saying this means anything in particular but I'm kind of excited about it," he continued. "Does anyone want to go see?"

Uh, yeah! Doug and I hurried down to Ryan's room and talked to our son. We saw more eye twitches, then Doug felt Ryan's leg move. We talked more excitedly to Ryan, trying to make contact with him and encourage him to fight harder. We saw a slight side-to-side rotation of his head.

Then Doug said, "Ryan, move your leg." And up his leg went! We stayed a little longer and I even saw his little toe curl. We thanked Ryan, over and over, for trying so hard. I hugged the nurse, and as Doug and I walked out through the big double doors of the ICU, we looked at each other. As our eyes met, we broke down crying and embraced. We felt hope, and right then and there we committed to standing together, as Ryan's parents, in full faith that he would be healed.

I wrote in my journal,

Thank you, Lord, for the grace you give us to make it through each day. We leave Ryan in your loving hands and ask you, the Great Physician, to finish what you've started. Hallelujah. Amen.

By the next day, Ryan was stable enough to be moved to another floor for the long-awaited CAT scan to his brain and body, and the first results were cause for rejoicing. Dr. Vespa said that while there was widespread brain damage, there was no obvious damage to the brain stem, the part of the brain that controls breathing, arousal and consciousness, attention and concentration, heart rate, and sleep and wake cycles. Good news.

And the news on the body scan was even better—another doctor from the trauma team told us he and his team were cautiously optimistic that Ryan could recover from all the injuries to his body—even his lungs! His body was beginning to recover. *Thank you, doctors. Thank you, Ryan. Thank you, Lord!*

CHAPTER 9

AT THE RED SEA

The body is just a shell for the spirit. It's temporary,
but the soul is eternal. . . . Your desire for God
must be so strong that you would be willing to lose
everything in this world to be with him in the next.

FROM RYAN'S SCREENPLAY

IT HAD BEEN TWO WEEKS since Ryan's accident, and I began to measure my days in small victories: Ryan's nostrils flaring as he began to take more breaths on his own. A cough here. A hiccup there. Even when he passed gas—these were all small signs of life, of a body beginning to recover and maybe, someday, wake up.

I began to write more and more often in the journal Jessi gave me:

> *I feel a change inside. Am I adjusting into a sense of*
> *security that Ryan will live? Am I starting to feel the*
> *reality of my new routine? I feel okay about sleeping at*
> *my parents' house now instead of in the visitor's lounge.*
> *And I'm realizing that as time goes by there will be fewer*
> *and fewer people with me. Doug and Mike will have to*
> *go back to work, Tyler to school, and Jessi to San Francisco.*
> *Debby has to get busy with her upcoming show in Branson*
> *and get her girls ready to leave for college. That's good in*
> *some ways so I can read and write and concentrate on*

*Ryan without saying the same things over and over to
caring visitors.*

*I foresee Mama and me holding down the fort
and sometimes, probably, just me. It's okay. I love to
be with him and talk and sing and read to him. I'm
getting less afraid to spend longer stretches of time
with him.*

Ryan's fiancée, Kristen, had begun to fear that Ryan might
not remember her when he came out of his coma. Ryan was
unaware of this, but Kristen's heart must have been broken,
her dreams in pieces.

It had to have felt like a long nightmare for Kristen as she
came to grips with the realization that, even if he did wake
up, Ryan might not remember dating her, falling in love with
her, or making plans with her for the future. I wasn't too worried that Ryan might not remember me. Even if he didn't, as
his mother I would always love him.

*I will let these thoughts go for now. We really don't know
anything about what Ryan will know or not know; be able
to do or not do. It could be a fast or slow recovery. It's in
the Lord's hands and either way, we have to praise him for
answering our prayers. Ryan lives and while he lives, there
is hope.*

Ryan had now been in a coma for about two weeks, and
his body couldn't seem to shake a nagging fever. Doctors
thought it a common infection from the accident or the
many surgical treatments and interventions. Despite heavy

doses of antibiotics, the fever continued. Doctors went ahead with their plans for surgery to insert a feeding tube, perform a tracheotomy so he could breathe more easily, clean out his sinuses to help fight infection, and begin repairing his heavily damaged jaw.

The morning of the surgery, I read this in Psalm 40:

I waited patiently for God to help me; then he listened and heard my cry. He lifted me out of the pit of despair, out from the bog and the mire, and set my feet on a hard, firm path, and steadied me as I walked along. He has given me a new song to sing, of praises to our God. Now many will hear of the glorious things he did for me, and stand in awe before the Lord, and put their trust in him. (vv. 1-3, TLB)

That last sentence hit me: "Many will hear. . . ." I remembered the first morning when I met with the Lord and he reminded me how Lazarus's illness was used for the glory of God. I wrote:

We often suffer the consequences of our own actions; trouble comes because we haven't done what we know we ought to do. But there are cases where a person has an accident, a freak accident, and we wrestle with why it happened.

Why had this accident happened to Ryan? Maybe God was giving me a little glimpse of his plan. I worked out my thoughts and feelings about this in my journal:

Maybe something like Ryan's accident is allowed by him, not caused by him, so that the glory of the Lord can be seen more clearly. Perhaps through it people will come to trust in him, that he is who he says he is and has the power to forgive sins.

After all, that's the bigger issue. The grace of God to forgive our sins is the bigger issue that matters beyond our lifetime and in order to get our attention, God does miracles. Once he has our attention and awe, he can deal with the issues of the heart.

I had recently reread the story of the friends who were so determined that their paralyzed friend see Jesus that they cut a hole in a roof and lowered the man on a mat, directly in front of him. Jesus, who was teaching to a packed house, looked at the paralytic and said, "Your sins are forgiven" (Luke 5:20). I believe Jesus had examined the man's heart and determined that was his biggest need. Of course, it is the biggest need of us all.

Though they said nothing, the religious leaders there that day were furious. *How dare Jesus claim God's authority and tell the man he was forgiven?* I love Jesus' answer in verses 22-24, and I wrote in my journal:

Jesus said in Luke 5, "What is harder, to forgive sins or heal the sick?" Then he went on to heal a lame man "so that you'll know I have the authority to forgive sins."

"Stand up, pick up your mat, and go home!" Jesus told the paralytic. The Gospel writer tells us that "immediately, as everyone watched, the man jumped up, picked up his mat, and went home praising God" (verses 24-25). That man was healed, not only so his life could be turned around, but as a way to authenticate Jesus' claim that he has the authority to forgive and save us.

Likewise, I believed then, and still believe now, that Ryan is being healed and restored to full function to demonstrate that Jesus is who he said he is. And if he can heal Ryan of all these injuries, he is also able to give grace and forgiveness to anyone who puts their faith in him. One commentary I read on Psalm 40 said this: "Often blessings cannot be received unless we go through the trial of waiting."[16]

Waiting. That described my life. As Ryan was wheeled into surgery, Doug followed in case more signatures were needed. Mama, Debby, and I stayed behind in the waiting room. We prayed and sang from hymnals Debby had brought. I was so grateful she brought them and marveled at how much the words to old hymns like "Blessed Assurance" and "It Is Well with My Soul" meant to me now. Daddy arrived and added his bass voice to our trio, and then Doug came back and joined in too.

Singing the hymns lifted me into God's presence, where I needed to be. All is well in the presence of God. It's like when you're a child and scared of thunder. If you can be in the same room with your parents who aren't afraid and who tell you everything is fine, then you're okay. I needed to be in God's room and hear him telling me not to fear and that everything was going to be fine.

It was a long wait, but finally, after an eleven-hour surgery, Dr. Charles Chandler came in to give us an update. Ryan's jaw had been fractured in four places so they had installed a steel plate with ten screws and rubber-banded his mouth shut so it could heal. The rest of the procedures went well, but I decided not to go see Ryan that night. I knew he would look different again with his face swollen and a tube in his throat. I needed sleep to be ready to face him.

When I woke up the next morning, these words ran through my mind: *Don't be afraid to go and see Ryan. I am with him and he's not in pain.* When I did see him, I was so focused on his face that for a long time I didn't even notice the tracheotomy tube in his throat.

When Dr. Chandler came in to check on Ryan, he clapped his hands loudly above Ryan's ear. Because Ryan reacted, the doctor thought Ryan could hear. I wanted more, but I praised Jesus for one miracle that day.

The hope we felt from that sign of Ryan's increasing awareness was tempered a few weeks later when his body began storming. People with traumatic brain injury can experience an exaggerated stress response due to an increase in activity of the sympathetic nervous system, which controls bodily functions like heart rate, respiration, and perspiration, particularly during the "fight or flight" response to stress.

Storming is involuntary, and in Ryan it led to his body's inability to regulate its temperature. Once his initial fever was finally gone, his temperature started to dip below normal. But as it dropped, he began to sweat as if he were in a sauna. As soon as we wiped him dry, beads of sweat began to form again. It was impossible to keep his bedclothes dry.

When his temperature began to come back up, it climbed too high. His bed was soaked with sweat, and his vital signs became erratic. His pulse and blood pressure went too high, and he breathed rapidly. It was particularly scary since the storming began on a Friday when none of his doctors were around. By Sunday, I felt like I was going to break. I felt a tremendous physical pressure in my chest, and I wondered whether I should ask my own doctor for some medication to give me relief. Inwardly I was pleading with God to *do something!*

Then, as Mike drove me home that night, I had a sweet experience. It was so unusual that, as I look back, I believe it was a special grace from God for that moment. I began to sense very strongly that Ryan himself had gotten permission from the Lord to comfort me. Not audibly, but in my spirit, I heard Ryan's voice.

Mom, it's all right. I'm okay. Don't worry—that's just my body. That's not who I am. I'm with Jesus and I'm safe. I had the sensation of Ryan's own arms around me as I know he would have comforted me with his physical hug if he were able. I began to calm down.

The next day, a neurosurgeon explained that the ups and downs and changes in Ryan's vital signs weren't uncommon to brain-injured patients. He assured us that this was not a life-and-death situation and that various medications could be used to manage the various symptoms. Ryan's biggest risk factors were infection and blood clots. The body is not meant to be immobile, and even though he was in a coma, Ryan needed to start moving, the doctor said.

I wrote in my journal:

I can't wait for physical therapy to begin.

As I look back, I can feel those intense feelings of helplessness and fear again. There were some good days like my Jericho run day, but there were plenty of dark days, including that first weekend of Ryan's storming. Then, and in the future when complications set in, there were moments when it looked like Ryan might not make it after all. But through it all I continued to hold on to a gut feeling I couldn't explain or justify—that this wasn't the end of Ryan's life but instead the beginning of a great ministry.

✦ ✦ ✦

Then we received a call from the Larry King show.

For a time, Larry King truly was the king of television. His show aired from the CNN studios in Los Angeles from 1985 to 2010. It was CNN's most watched program, with millions of viewers around the world on CNN International. Larry interviewed at least one high-profile person a night, ranging from Hollywood celebrities to newsmakers to ordinary individuals with a compelling story to tell. Some of his most notable guests over the years included Mario Cuomo (his first guest), Oprah Winfrey, Barbara Walters, Marlon Brando, Jerry Seinfeld, President Bill Clinton, and President Barack Obama.

What I didn't know was that Daddy and Larry were old friends. Daddy first knew Larry early on when he was doing a local talk radio show in Miami, at a desk in a hotel lounge. Larry interviewed Daddy and they had an instant liking for each other. After Larry's radio show went national in 1978, Daddy was on his show several times. "He was a semi-fan," Daddy joked.

So Daddy wasn't too surprised when he got a call from Larry's producer shortly after Ryan's accident. The producer said Larry had heard about Ryan's accident on the news and wanted Daddy and me to come on the show for a few minutes so that people would hear about Ryan's accident and pray for him. Even though Daddy wasn't surprised by the call, he thought the reason for the invitation was extraordinary. "He's giving us a platform," he said.

I wasn't sure I could do it. Going on television to talk about Ryan's accident struck me as being in bad taste. "I feel too raw. I am a gaping wound. How do I talk about this in public? It's all too horrible."

But we decided to accept the invitation. Ryan needed every prayer he could get.

Larry was famously agnostic. He was extraordinarily open minded and often plied people of faith with penetrating questions about their beliefs. Larry was curious about the nature of God but said he hadn't been able to personally connect to God. At one point early in their acquaintance, Daddy had a brief faith conversation with him and said, "Larry, I don't have all the answers, but I'd love to sit down and talk to you sometime." Larry had given him the phone number of his Washington, DC, apartment, but Daddy was rarely in town and had never used it. Now Larry had called him in and they were about to have that long-promised conversation about faith. In front of millions.

Daddy and I made our first appearance on *Larry King Live* on July 26, 2001. It had been five weeks since Ryan's accident. He was alive but hadn't progressed much and was still lying, comatose, in a bed at UCLA Medical Center.

A good friend of Daddy's—someone he'd known since he was a teenager—accompanied us. His name is Kenneth Copeland, and he is a preacher and television show host from Texas. When Daddy first knew him, however, Kenneth was a rowdy football player. Mike came along and waited for me in the Green Room.

I think I was still in shock, but all I could think about as the lights came on and Larry took his seat across the table from Daddy, Kenneth, and me was the story of Lazarus and Jesus praying so others would believe and God would be glorified. I was on the Larry King show so others would hear and believe.

While sitting on the set felt surreal, I was calm. By this time I was living in total dependence on the Holy Spirit to make it through each day. I had prayed for strength and the words God wanted me to say. I knew countless people would be impacted by the way my family and I responded to pressure, how we reacted when things had gone so terribly wrong.

Larry started by asking the details of the accident and Daddy told the story of Ryan's fall. He told Larry that even though we were grieving and we didn't know what to expect, we were trusting God. Daddy said that we were praying, that we had our churches and prayer chains praying and fasting, and that Ryan was "bathed in prayer." He also shared the story of Mama's continuing prayer: "He will not die. He will live and testify to the glory of God."

I spoke up and told Larry how I talked to Ryan, sang to him, and read Scripture to him. When Larry asked if I was angry with God, I explained that I was actually clinging to God, crying out to him, "Lord, talk to me. I need you."

After Larry broke to a commercial, Larry's producers

showed a brief clip from a twenty-year-old video of Daddy holding Ryan as a little boy as he, Mama, my sisters, and I sang "Let It Begin with Me."

Daddy ended our ten-minute appearance with a powerful statement of his personal faith. He spoke for me, too, when he said, "We're not camped in the valley of the shadow of death. We're going *through* it." Then he looked into the camera and asked everyone to pray for Ryan.

We went home, exhausted. I needed rest so I could get up the next morning and get back to the hospital. While I appreciated the chance to be on the show and ask people to pray for Ryan, I was so busy I didn't think much more about it. But other people did. The response was immediate and amazing. The phones at CNN rang off the hook. Over the next few weeks, thousands of letters and e-mails deluged the studio. Here's a sampling of some of the messages we received:

> *Let me first start by telling you I was Ryan's boss in Newport Beach. I hired Ryan and trained him. He was a pleasure to be around. We became friends. I remember the day he got into Pepperdine. I knew back then as I am sure still to this day that Ryan will contribute something great to our world.*

✦

> *Hi, Ryan. I saw your story on CNN's Larry King Live. My name is Argy and I'm from Athens, Greece. I'm really touched by your story. Deep down I know that not only will you get okay but you'll also play basketball again.*

✦

I am an Arabic girl and the first time I know Ryan is from Larry King Live. When I saw him I felt my heart crying, not my eyes.

✦

Please tell Ryan we pray for him and that we expect results from God and we will not let up until Ryan is healed.

✦

Thank you for letting us see that famous families have the same difficulties as people who will never be household words. In fact, I think in some ways it must be more difficult at times because you have to put on a brave front for the public. . . . God still has a lot for Ryan to do.

✦

I'm sorry for the grief and trials your family is going through, but now God can make Ryan into someone special. . . . One day Ryan will be mighty. He is going to be mighty in God's eyes regardless of whatever physical state he is in.

✦

In the name of Jesus, rise up, Ryan.

✦ ✦ ✦

At the end of July, the UCLA doctors decided Ryan was ready to be transferred from the hospital to a subacute care facility because he no longer needed the intensive care that had kept him alive at first. I was nervous but excited. Everyone agreed that we'd start Ryan at New Orange Hills, a care and rehabilitation facility in the city of Orange, south of Los Angeles.

Ryan was placed in a private room and our family loved having a whole room to ourselves. We even had a window!

Even after his move, the only time I would leave Ryan's side was when someone else agreed to stay with him. He was still so fragile and needed constant monitoring. Friends and family members graciously volunteered, and every night, someone stayed awake in the room with Ryan. I didn't know how long I could continue to ask friends for this kind of help.

Shortly after Ryan was admitted, I had to sit through another pessimistic doctor meeting. Following that I wrote,

The new doctor told us all the same negative stuff. I won't even write it down. The most important thing is that Ryan has been improving. He hasn't been on the respirator at all and a physical therapist is helping improve his range of motion.

Even though Ryan was still in a coma, on the second day at New Orange Hills, the nursing staff dressed him and put him in a chair. They wanted to get him off his back. Mama, Ryan, and I sat outside for thirty minutes, enjoying some fresh air together for the first time in over six weeks. But there was a warning sign—this simple activity that made us so happy caused him to start sweating. When his heart rate went up, we had to take him inside and get him back in bed.

A week later, Ryan began to storm again, and he sweated profusely from seven at night to five the following morning. He demonstrated abnormal posturing, another classic sign of storming. His muscles were involuntarily rigid and contracting, and his head was turned to the side, teeth grinding, eyes wide open. Mama stayed with him all that night, never sleeping so she could wipe away his sweat and change his hospital gown when it got soaked.

When I arrived the next morning, Ryan had a temperature of 104. As frightening as that was, I was even more frightened by Ryan's appearance. He had lost so much water overnight that he looked like a skeleton. Mama looked exhausted and apologetic, as if this was somehow her fault.

Ryan seemed in grave danger. I called Daddy to ask him to pray, and Mike and Doug to ask them to come. I tried to make Mama go get some sleep but she wouldn't leave. The staff was working with Ryan, so I drove to get a muffin and some coffee for Mama. When I got back, I rubbed her swollen ankles. I was afraid she would collapse.

Ryan's body relaxed and seemed to calm down after he had been hydrated, but a few days later he began another storming session that lasted twenty hours with no break. Finally, at 3 a.m., the staff decided to move him to the intensive care unit at Chapman Medical, a nearby hospital. This time, Ryan's temperature was 106.

The nurses left him completely naked to allow his body to cool off but he was dehydrated, just skin and bones. Seeing him lying exposed on a table, thin beyond recognition, knowing everything he had been through, made me want to run away. I collapsed in a chair, defeated and wishing it would all stop. I was in a panic. It was a nightmare situation and I felt there must be something more we could do.

While Daddy and Doug were in an intense discussion

with the neurologist and the trauma internist about the possibility of transferring him to another facility, I retreated to a small waiting room. Mama came with me. I was curled up in a chair, quietly waiting. I didn't think I could take much more. I couldn't cry and I felt empty, unable to reach out to God. I was starting to wonder if any of it did any good. My faith was depleted and my fight was gone.

"I know God won't give us more than we can bear," I told my mom, "but I don't think I can bear any more." Mama didn't know what else to do but pray, so she put her hands on me and prayed when I could not.

Finally Doug and Daddy came back, encouraged. Ryan had somehow stopped sweating. He relaxed and his temperature had gone down to 101. They felt he was in good hands there at Chapman and the doctors had held out some hope—although the odds weren't with Ryan, people in his condition had been known to recover from brain storming.

I finally wept. The storming episode had been so long, my doubts so great, and my sleep so little that I was broken. I didn't want my beautiful son to see me in this sad state so I just sat nearby, waiting.

Forgive me, Lord, for shutting you out. I know you know my heart. I am proclaiming your sovereignty but sometimes I want to take things into my own hands. I have such a helpless feeling and I don't know if I can bear what you have in store. Please bring us something to encourage us. Give me a deeper trust. Don't let me waste an opportunity to represent you to others.

Two days later Ryan was transferred to Mission Hospital in Mission Viejo, just fifteen minutes from our house. Brian Flynn, one of the paramedics who helped transport Ryan there, turned out to be a friend of his. They'd played basketball together at Irvine High School. Later we learned that he had also been through a head trauma and had undergone eight months of rehabilitation. He was fit, strong, and whole. That was the encouragement I was looking for.

✦ ✦ ✦

On August 17, Daddy, Kenneth Copeland, and I were invited back on *Larry King Live*, this time for a whole hour. Joining us were Max Lucado, author and pastor, and Dave Owen, Ryan's pastor from the Malibu Vineyard Church.

Larry started off talking about the huge response around the world following our first appearance on the show. People had not only called his television studio, they'd called the hospital as well, trying to find out how Ryan was doing. Doug had set up a special phone hotline where he recorded daily updates on Ryan's condition. Larry gave out the number to viewers (probably hoping they'd stop calling his studio!).

"People are hungry to know if prayer really works," Larry said thoughtfully. He had us tell the story of the accident again and asked for any progress. We joyfully shared some small victories. Recently Ryan's eyes had opened. He could blink, though not on command. Occasionally his eyes would focus and follow movement for a brief time.

I told Larry how I coped. "I rely heavily on what [God] says in his Word more now than ever before," I said. I read a verse about how "endurance develops strength"[17] and said I was learning patience as I waited for God to heal Ryan.

"Ryan's at the Red Sea, and we're having to wait like Moses," Daddy added.[18]

Larry listened, friendly and sympathetic. He asked about talking to Ryan and whether we felt we were getting through. "We talk to Ryan's spirit," Daddy said.

I was much bolder this time. "The Lord has been walking me through this day by day," I said, even though I was frustrated by the circumstances of Ryan's recent battle with storming.

Then Larry welcomed a caller, who asked us the million-dollar question. Essentially, he asked, "What if Ryan doesn't come out of the coma? How will that affect the faith of you and your family?"

It was a powerful moment. I felt like millions of viewers around the world sucked in their breath, leaned forward, and listened.

Daddy answered. The words came easy because they were true and real. He said God is in charge. He will work it for good. And because we have eternal life through Christ, we have hope.

"We've already seen the first miracle," he said. "Ryan is alive."

✦ ✦ ✦

Here are more responses from Larry's viewers:

How good it was to see you all again on the Larry King show. I have been praying for Ryan ever since I heard of his injury.

✦

*I admire how your family is dealing with this problem.
I really, really believe that the reason God answered
your prayer is that you never gave up hope. You always
believed Ryan would get better.*

✦

*Ryan, please know that you are going to make it. Doctors
are very smart people, but they quite often can't see the
whole picture. Your destiny lies in your hands and God's.
What a powerful combination!*

✦

*I'm glad I can type this because after watching Larry King
tonight I am practically speechless! The power of prayer
is so awesome, and I am so thrilled to see the progress
Ryan has made. There is no doubt in my mind that this
beautiful young man will indeed be a guest of Larry's
sometime in the future.*

CHAPTER 10

THE SECRET TENT

I can show you hope. I can open your eyes to a secret and a mystery
that would change the way you see the world and everyone in it.

FROM RYAN'S SCREENPLAY

I WAS DETERMINED to be strong and brave, and for the most part I was full of faith, but after a while the day-to-day hospital existence began to wear me down. Fatigue set in. Bone-deep, heartsick fatigue. I wanted to have my old life back. Not just my son, but my life.

On a typical day, I got to the hospital at 9 a.m. I had tried getting there earlier, only to discover that because the nurses were changing shifts and getting Ryan cleaned up, I usually couldn't go into his room until 9 anyway.

Ryan wasn't responding yet at all. His eyes, though usually open, were vacant. That didn't prevent me from doing everything I could to reach him. I spent my days singing or talking to Ryan, massaging his hands and feet, and working through some range-of-motion exercises with him. Sometimes I'd read to him or even turn the TV on to a program I thought he would like. I also spent a lot of time talking with Ryan's caregivers, letting them know what an incredible guy he was in the hopes that they would care about Ryan, too, and do whatever they could to make him comfortable. I stayed six hours, until 3 p.m., then left to run errands and spend some time in the evenings with Mike and Tyler.

I was able to have that much time away from the hospital only because my sweet, devoted mother was living in a hotel so she could come to the hospital every day too. She rarely spent a night in her own bed. Mama usually arrived at one in the afternoon; then we'd spend a couple of hours together with Ryan. The only reason I was able to tear myself away from Ryan was because I knew having my mom with him was the closest thing to having me there. Ryan adores my mom and she adores him.

After Mama left at seven, Mike, Jessi, Doug, Vic, or another family member or friend sat with Ryan until ten. And Daddy, even with his busy schedule and many commitments, visited Ryan almost every weekend.

During the late night and early morning hours, a caregiver, paid for by my parents, sat in Ryan's room watching, communicating with the staff, and taking notes for me when anything out of the ordinary happened. This was the only way I could get any sleep at night. The thought of Ryan being left alone in his room without help would have kept me awake at night and I would've had to stay there myself.

Ten weeks after Ryan's accident and just days after I'd been on *Larry King Live* for the second time proclaiming my faith in a healing God and telling the world I believed Ryan would get better, I started losing hope. I wasn't seeing anything new. I wrote,

I'm starting to feel that if God were going to restore Ryan, we would have come further than this by now. If I lose

hope in Ryan's healing, I think I will lose so much more than that—I will lose my ability to ever enjoy anything again.

I feel resentful when I see anyone else in my family enjoy anything. I can't feel pleasure in anything. I don't feel pleasure in seeing friends. They want to console me and I've heard it all now and it's beginning to sound like futile words. I can only be consoled by these words: "Ryan is awake."

Ryan's recovery sometimes felt like a slow roller coaster ride, with moments to celebrate at the top of the hill, and those desperate moments when I felt like I was flung down into deep despair, wondering if he would ever wake up. Those ups and downs, the tension and decisions, the bad news and test results, the changes in facilities and caregivers, all took a toll on me.

If he doesn't smile again, I don't think I'll ever be able to.

From the moment I first walked into UCLA Medical Center after returning from Spain, my priorities had changed. I fixed all my energy and focus on helping Ryan recover, and my other responsibilities melted into the background. As the summer drew to a close, I felt myself wearing down, and I was unable to give enough attention to Mike, Jessi, or Tyler. My whole world revolved around Ryan and his needs. And I was broken.

At the very end of August, I reached the point of feeling like I couldn't go on. One morning as I stood in front of my bathroom sink getting ready to go to the hospital again, I was overwhelmed with grief. My tears became groans and suddenly my groans became screams. I'd never felt such grief or even witnessed it in someone else. I stuffed a washcloth in my mouth, trying to stifle the awful sounds. It didn't work. Mike came in and put his arms around me.

"If Ryan doesn't get better, I'll never survive," I gasped out between sobs. "I'll never have a reason to smile again for the rest of my life."

Mike told me to breathe deep. "We'll make it through this," he said.

"I won't make it," I cried.

"Stop talking that way," he said.

"Get off me," I shouted, suddenly angry, as I tried to squirm out of his arms. "Nobody can tell me I'll recover from this."

I was undone. I stopped screaming and struggling and went numb. I felt nothing and had no expression on my face at all. I tried to get dressed and fix my hair so I could go to the hospital, though I didn't really care how I looked. I felt ugly and tired and sad. I finally dragged myself to the hospital, but I couldn't make myself go to see Ryan, so I stayed in the waiting room. I kept asking others how he was doing, only to start crying again. I knew I couldn't bear to be with Ryan right then.

Later that day, Mike asked if I wanted to see a doctor to get some help. I said yes, mainly for Tyler's sake.

I love Tyler and I don't want to be crazy. I love everyone else too, but I feel like they will understand and can excuse me for being crazy right now. But Tyler is just a kid. He could be confused and permanently damaged if I don't get it together.

That same day I saw a nurse-practitioner who prescribed Prozac and Xanax. I took one Xanax for anxiety when I got home that night, which helped me calm down. The next day I started on Prozac and stayed home alone, taking a day off from the hospital. I felt relieved to have permission to run away, if just for a day, from my horrible reality.

I haven't felt like reaching out to God much but I am anyway. I'm listening for his voice but feeling like maybe I'm wasting my time.

I tried to relax in my bed but phone calls and visitors kept me from sleeping. I watched a Christian television show about a man who'd experienced sudden healing from a serious condition that had seemed as if it would result in amputation. As I look back, I realize that on one of the most difficult days of my life, with my faith holding on by a thread, God used that man's story to plant a tiny seed of hope in my heart.

Then, at 5 p.m., someone tapped on my bedroom door. It opened and I looked up, expecting Jessi. Instead, my sister Laury was peeking in to see if I was sleeping. I jumped out of bed and hugged her. Mike had flown her in from Colorado to spend a few days with me. Laury's empathetic, soothing personality was wonderful, better than any medication. She was fresh to the situation. It hadn't worn her down yet, so she was able to absorb some of the sadness.

I felt so loved by my husband, and it touched me so deeply that he had taken the time and effort to bring her to me. Mama joined us when we went out to dinner, and by the end of the evening, I started to feel human again.

I need my loved ones so much to help me through this.
I don't want to become bitter and lose touch with God.
I don't want to lose all hope. I am floundering between
faith and despair.

✦ ✦ ✦

When the fatigue set in, so did the fighting. I wish I could say I always reacted in love or that my faith was unshakable during the moments of disagreement, anger, and frustration, but that wouldn't be true. I'm willing to share the moments I'm not proud of because it might help others who are going through something similar.

For example, when I first said I wanted a caregiver in Ryan's room at night, Mama thought it was a good idea but Mike disagreed. He thought it would be a huge waste of money because the facility's professionals were perfectly able to take care of Ryan. He told me I was being overprotective to think Ryan needed eyes on him around the clock. To me, hospitals seemed understaffed and the staff overworked. I was afraid they would make mistakes.

At the time, I wanted Mike to see it the way I did, and it broke my heart when he didn't. Mike, on the other hand, was looking at the situation from a more practical standpoint. How much money was it going to take to care for Ryan for the rest of his life? Shouldn't we start planning for the future? What if we needed that money later for some sort of care more important than this?

I felt that if Mike only understood the depths of my need to make sure Ryan had everything possible to keep him safe, he would not have fought me on this. In the end he resigned himself to the extra caregiver. All I know is that for me, there *was* no decision to make. Ryan needed to have this extra help in place. There was money to pay for it. Done.

Years later, Mike had a change of heart about this. I heard him counseling a young man whose wife had suffered a brain injury. Mike explained to him the importance of being an advocate for a loved one because hospital staff can make mistakes and overlook things.

Whenever I pushed Mike or anyone else to do something, I did so because I felt like I was acting in Ryan's best interest. I was under enormous stress, but I was consumed with doing whatever had to be done to make sure my son was safe and had every possible chance to recover. If anyone had a different point of view, look out!

In an ideal world, nobody would ever be left unattended in a hospital bed. But the reality is that many people don't have the money to pay for an extra caregiver, so hiring one would never even be considered. I share the dilemma we faced because it's an example of how people who love each other can disagree so strongly. We all do the best we can and then leave the rest to God.

And the reality is that Mike was committed to making things work, and he was a rock, the stable force that could handle things I didn't know how to do. He made sure I was okay and that Tyler was taken care of when I was immersed in Ryan's care, sometimes ignoring my husband and my other two children.

About six months after Ryan's accident, Jessi came to me, distraught. She had quit her job in San Francisco and moved back to Southern California to help. Up to this point, she had been strong and positive, so when she came to me and tried to explain that she was starting to lose her way, I didn't understand the depth of it. She cried and I said, "You're going to be fine. You have your whole life ahead of you." I didn't know she'd been forcing a positive attitude to help me cope while she was falling apart. I didn't recognize that she was sinking into a serious and deep depression. Instead, I thought it had something to do with the job change and the move. I said, "Can I worry about you next year?" She told me later she felt like I pulled the rug out from under her and she was falling through the air with no ground in sight.

Since then, we've discovered we are very different. Jessi is very intuitive and can almost feel what a person is thinking. I, on the other hand, am not as complicated. I easily let people know what I need because I figure that's the only way they will know. But because Jessi can tell immediately if something is wrong with someone she loves, she expected that I could too. She didn't clearly articulate everything she was feeling but thought that as her mother I would naturally recognize that she was drowning in despair and she needed me to tune into her as much as I was to Ryan. My reaction, or lack thereof, made her feel like she was on her own.

I'm not proud of that moment. Jessi felt like I'd abandoned her, and my question created a serious wound that, when I finally understood, took years of care and communication to begin to heal. I adore my daughter, and over time we have come to appreciate our differences. I've learned so much from her. I've often told her I want to be like her when I grow up.

✦ ✦ ✦

Despite many dark days, I realize now that, time and again, just when I felt I'd been stretched as far as I could endure, something new would happen to bring relief and joy. On Labor Day 2001, that something new was chocolate pudding.

Never in my wildest dreams did I ever think I'd celebrate any child of mine eating a fatty, sugary dessert. Like my parents and my sisters, I've always been conscious of what food I eat, trying to maintain a healthy, balanced diet with lots of fresh fruits and veggies. Daddy modeled both a desire to eat green, leafy stuff as well as a sweet tooth. In order to counter the sweet tooth, it's important to me that I get some exercise every day. I've always made it a priority to get up early and go for a jog or stop in at the gym for a workout. I still work out six days a week, and for several years I've taught exercise classes at local gyms. So greasy fast food wasn't usually on the daily family menu. But Ryan needed to be able to eat. Tube feeding was keeping Ryan alive, but it was also a visible sign that he was unable to do something as basic as swallow a bite of food.

Ryan was making some progress. His broken jaw and his ribs healed. His internal organs were slowly recovering. His bruises and bumps were fading away. His eyes were open and I looked at each and every movement he made as a small victory. He would follow me with his eyes when I walked by his bed. A nurse wrote in his records that Ryan had responded to Jessi's voice at one point when he was gasping for air. She repeatedly spoke to him and his symptoms resolved. Another time, his fiancée felt him squeeze her hand. These were wonderful moments. But Ryan was still in a coma or a persistent vegetative state. His records said, "Patient has not been interactive with nurses or others." It's rare for a coma to last more than two to four weeks; most people either slowly recover or slowly decline. Ryan seemed to be hovering somewhere in between.

Therapists worked hard to keep his limbs and joints flexible and healthy. I wanted Ryan to remember how to smile so I physically turned his lips up to remind him—maybe when moved passively the muscles would remember how to move actively.

Another problem was the danger of infection. For someone in a persistent vegetative state, the most common cause of death is infection, such as pneumonia.[19] During the months after his surgery, Ryan struggled with several infections, including deadly staph infections and bouts with pneumonia. At times he was kept in isolation, and to visit him we had to wear masks, gowns, and rubber gloves. It was also a constant battle to keep his skin healthy and free of bedsores, which can lead to serious infection, so with the help of nurses, we had him sitting upright in chairs as much as possible to relieve pressure on his skin.

So after the storming and the infections, his reaction to chocolate pudding was something to shout about. Can you imagine not eating anything for several months, then tasting a mouthful of chocolate pudding? Imagine the cool creamy texture hitting your tongue, the sweet, rich flavor coating the roof of your mouth, and then the cold sensation of the pudding sliding down your throat.

Ryan finally got to experience that. Even though he wasn't fully awake yet, his eyes were open, so Jessi decided to try taste stimulation with some chocolate pudding she had brought. She put on a rubber glove and dabbed some pudding on her finger. Then she tried to coax Ryan to put it on his tongue. After some of his usual random, agitated movement, he stilled his head and with great concentration, he opened his mouth. She dabbed the pudding on his tongue and he licked his lips and swallowed.

We all gasped, amazed. "Ryan, do you want more?" Jessi asked.

He moved his head back and forth, a rhythmic movement that seemed to be automatic. Then he gradually stopped moving and opened his mouth again. Jessi put more pudding on his tongue. Then he did it three more times. We were so excited! The chocolate pudding incident meant Ryan had reached four important milestones: He heard us, he understood enough to open his mouth, he was able to open his mouth, and he could taste the pudding.

On September 5, Ryan was moved from Mission Hospital, where he had been for three weeks, to St. Jude Medical Center for their coma stimulation program. Though it was a much longer drive for us to St. Jude than it had been to Mission Hospital, he would now receive physical therapy, occupational therapy, and speech therapy every day.

I'm happy he was accepted at St. Jude. I wish the move were tomorrow instead of today, though. Tyler starts school tomorrow. Today is his last day of summer. I wish we could have planned something fun for him to do. Instead, he'll stay home alone until Mike can pick him up at noon and bring him to the hospital. I haven't spent any time with Tyler for the last two days and I miss him. On top of everything else, Jessi leaves for New York on business today. She'll be gone for five days and I won't have her smiling face and extra help. So I didn't sleep well. I got up early and the first thing I read in my devotional book by Max Lucado was the heading, "Don't Panic." I felt like it was directed at me. And so was the verse: "Let us hold firmly to the hope that we have confessed, because we can trust God to do what he promised" (Hebrews 10:23).[20] Okay, Lord. I'm trusting you today.

Jessi returned from New York on September 10, and the next morning, we were watching the news together before leaving for the hospital. We watched as smoke billowed from the Twin Towers to the sky, and right before the towers fell, Jessi said, "Mom, I was just there! I was standing outside looking at them yesterday. What if this had happened then?" I was so glad she had made it home. If she had been hurt or even stranded, I don't know what I would have done.

As I sat with Ryan that day, watching the horrific events of 9/11 unfold on TV, I knew the world was changing. I knew numerous families were now enveloped in the fog of grief, not knowing what to do next, just as I had felt three months before. I imagined thousands of family members and friends of the lost groaning and screaming as I had in my room only weeks ago.

Then I remembered that Ryan had talked about

prophecy when he came back from Hawaii. His passion for the topic had been ignited while he was doing so much reading and research for his screenplay. His roommate Steve told me that Ryan had talked about Old Testament prophecy pointing to an event that would be an attack on American soil. His friends had grown tired of Ryan harping on the subject and told him to "chill out." Even Kristen had been nervous, wondering if he was going too far and might offend someone.

That September 11, I was wishing I had paid better attention to what Ryan had told me. I wished I had his notes and could find the Bible book, chapter, and verse that led him to those provocative conclusions. I wished he were able to wake up and discuss these things with me again. What would have been his reaction to the shocking news of that day?

✦ ✦ ✦

Every day as I sat by Ryan's bed, I watched carefully for changes that might signal recovery. One unusual thing I'd noticed was that, since the accident, Ryan had never turned his head to the right side on his own. He always moved his head to the left. His eyes always looked to the left too. This was a result of involuntary muscle contraction from the brain injury. Daddy had seen one of the MRIs of Ryan's brain. A normal brain looks grayish on an MRI and you can clearly see the folds and bends of the brain tissue. But Ryan's brain looked like it had a black lace doily over the top. The black lace was atrophied brain tissue. Dead zones. And one of those dead zones prevented him from consciously controlling the right side of his body.

So to remind him to begin using it, I started whispering in his ear, "Ryan, you have a right."

In my journal I wrote,

Not only does Ryan have a "right side," but he also has a right to good health, to speech, to movement, and to restoration. Ryan, you have a right!

We also have a right to a full and abundant life and to be everything God created us to be. Before man sinned, there was communion with God. There was no sickness, no disease. But sin entered the world and separated us from God. To bridge the gap, Jesus died to pay the price for man's sin. When we accept Jesus as the final sacrifice, the debt is paid and we are free. We have the right to be everything God created us to be. Ryan understood this more than most of us and accepted this free gift.

As I wrote this entry, I thought of a scene from Ryan's screenplay in which Yeshua (Jesus) talks about sharing the Good News he's come to proclaim: "Don't stop until the entire globe has had the chance to hear the message. Not everyone will want to hear it, and many people will hate you because of it. So deliver the message in love and with a spirit of freedom, but never give up or lose your faith. The fate of the world is dependent on you all standing up, maybe even giving your life . . . for me and the truth."

Yeshua's friend Pete responds, "You have no reason to believe me, but I want you to know that from this moment on, I only live for you. To my last breath, I'll make sure that the world knows, no matter what."

Ryan, you have a right. Remember your right!

A few days later, Ryan's face scrunched up like it did whenever the therapist was stretching his neck and shoulders, only nobody was working on him. Then Mike and I watched in amazement as he turned his head to the right. It looked painful, yet he did it all by himself. It was as if Jesus was doing what the therapist usually did. It gave me chills.

Another incredible moment happened one day when Ryan's dad was visiting. Mama, Daddy, and I went in the other room to let Doug have time alone with Ryan. The nurses had propped Ryan up in a wheelchair. Doug was ready to leave and leaned over to say good-bye and give Ryan a kiss on the cheek. As usual, his head was turned to the left. So Doug kissed him on the right cheek. Then Ryan pursed his lips and turned his head to the center. Doug, almost afraid to breathe, leaned closer, and Ryan gave his dad a kiss on the cheek.

Ryan still had a blank look in his eyes and almost no expression on his face, but Doug knew something amazing had just happened. His heart started beating hard, and he called us in. I thought maybe it was a random head movement and Doug just mistook it for a kiss. But with us all in the room this time, Doug showed us. Ryan deliberately placed his lips against Doug's cheek and kissed with a little kissing sound. We began to cry tears of joy, and one by one, we each asked Ryan for a kiss. Daddy, Mama, and me. He kissed each one of us. Then I started bawling joyful tears. It was bliss!

In his lifetime I had kissed Ryan hundreds and thousands of times, but this gentle kiss from my grown son was the most precious one of all. People in comas usually don't kiss. To me, that kiss meant Ryan, my loving, affectionate son, was waking up. It was the first really meaningful action he had taken to reach out and interact with us. Ryan was in that frozen body, and he was fighting to get out.

Another day I was walking into his room when he sneezed really loudly. It was the first sneeze since his accident, and it was a delightfully natural thing to see him do. It looked like he was going to sneeze again. But instead he drew a deep breath, paused, then let out a loud sigh. It took me a moment to realize that I'd heard his voice, his deep, sweet, man's voice. I burst into tears again. It was the most beautiful sound I've ever heard.

In November, Ryan turned twenty-five years old. He ate twenty-five tiny bites of ice cream. The writing on his cake said "Battle on, Ryan." My sister Cherry was in town and brought Ryan a gift she had made herself—a hand-knit afghan in Pepperdine's colors of blue, orange, and white. She'd made it extra big to cover Ryan's long legs. In the card, she wrote that every single stitch was a prayer.

November was also the month slated for Ryan and Kristen's wedding. Her wedding dress had been delivered a few weeks after the accident, and she had finally decided to return it. The honeymoon plans had been cancelled. One by one, every wedding decision she and Ryan had made had to be undone.

Kristen had reacted with amazing strength through the shock and initial losses following Ryan's accident, but over time her visits to Ryan were shorter and less frequent. I understood she was hurting, but if anyone in our family acted like their hurt took precedence over Ryan and his recovery, I judged them harshly. I felt the same about his fiancée.

One day that month while we had lunch together at the hospital, I intended to clear the air by talking with her about this. Instead our conversation turned into a painful conflict. The next day I realized I owed her an apology; I was wrong in how I spoke to her, and I unnecessarily hurt someone who was already so wounded. I sent her a letter in which I expressed my remorse, and we have been in contact a few times since then. Forgiveness has been expressed, although she hasn't come to see Ryan since the day our lunch went all wrong. I don't believe it's because we hold any bitterness, but because it must be so painful for her to see Ryan. Not long ago I learned that Kristen has married and is now a mother, and I couldn't be happier that she has found new love and family. I hope and pray we will see each other again someday so I can give her a big hug, look her in the eye, and tell her in person that I love her and am sorry.

✦ ✦ ✦

In late fall, the physical therapists began getting Ryan out of bed and lifting him to an upright position using a standing frame, an important therapy for nonambulatory patients. One day my sister Debby wrote me a beautiful note, inspired by an e-mail I had sent her about a session Ryan had with this hydraulic device. Debby has a way of perceiving deep truths in very ordinary places. I want to share with you what she wrote:

> *There was a sentence you wrote, Lindy, that froze in my mind, or maybe I should say, in my spirit. The therapist said, "It is good for his bones to feel the weight of his body." I don't know why it impacted me the way it did but I recognized the feeling. I knew there was some deep spiritual truth in those words but it was deeper than my understanding.*

Those words have been playing over and over in my thoughts for days. What do they mean? What are you trying to say to me, Lord? "It is good for his bones to feel the weight of his body."

I know the obvious. All our bones need to bear weight to be strengthened. I know we are all supposed to do weight-bearing exercise to prevent the loss of bone density as we get older. So Ryan, who has been lying flat for these months and not feeling any weight, not even his own body weight on his bones, would benefit from being lifted upright to feel the weight of his flesh.

Does he feel his frailty? His weakness? Does it hurt? Is it frightening? Does he realize that he cannot bear the weight of his own flesh without help?

Do we realize it? We are frail and weak. We are all of us in pain and we are all frightened. We cannot bear the weight of our own flesh without help.

Suddenly now, the image of sweet Ryan being lifted upright is transformed in my heart into the image of sweet Jesus being lifted up on a cross, bearing the weight of all our flesh, all our weakness, all our suffering—all the evil in the world and the pain it has inflicted—the four planes that went down on September 11 and all the people inside them—all those lost in the Twin Towers and the Pentagon, and the agony of loss for the loved ones left behind.

Unbearable grief, but he bore all of this and more than we will ever comprehend, at least in this life, so that we wouldn't have to bear it. At least not alone. And most of all, not without hope.

It is good for us to feel the weight of his body.

"For [His] strength and power are made perfect (fulfilled and completed) and show themselves most effective in [your] weakness. Therefore, I will all the more gladly glory in my weaknesses and infirmities, that the strength and power of Christ (the Messiah) may rest (yes, may pitch a tent over and dwell) upon [us]!" (2 Corinthians 12.9).[21]

This is the secret tent, Lindy, that we have been hiding in, the safe shelter where all we have ever needed or will need has been provided. So many times when I have been in my prayer closet I have had the most overwhelming sense that everything I bring to him there—all my pain, all my fear, all my failures— is behind him on the bones on that cross that bore the weight of his flesh, which bore all our burdens so that we wouldn't have to, at least not alone, and most of all, not without hope. I see his arms outstretched and I can almost feel them embrace me, and it is good to feel the weight of his body.

How blessed I was to have someone like Debby, who not only showed up to sit with me, but who shared in the desperate seeking. She spent time on her knees, in the Word, opening her heart to what the Word of the Lord spoke to her so she could share it with me. Debby was an open line through which God could get his message to me. He will do that with any of us when we give ourselves over to being in his presence, listening, seeking.

CHAPTER 11

THE HAPPY MEAL

The truth is here in front of you.
You just have to open your eyes to see it.

RYAN WAS BEATING the odds and making slow but steady progress. However, St. Jude couldn't keep Ryan any longer because his progress was too slow for the insurance company to continue to pay for his therapy. We found a residence facility not far from our home called CareMeridian, which cares for brain-injured patients and provides essential therapy. Our insurance didn't agree to pay for it at first. We weren't sure how long we could keep paying out of pocket for CareMeridian, and we weren't sure how long Ryan would need to be there. I wanted him to live at home as soon as possible.

One day shortly after Ryan was moved there, I was driving on the toll road when I saw the most beautiful full double rainbow arced over the canyon near CareMeridian. It excited me because I know God first used a rainbow to mark an important promise that he had made. I truly felt the significance of it and welled up with gratitude for this beautiful sign that Ryan was not out of God's sight.

Before Ryan transferred to CareMeridian, his trache tube

was finally removed. Yet, even though he was making gains, I felt darkness and sadness descending again as the holidays approached. I resented feeling like I had to participate this year. Christmas Eve was our wedding anniversary, and we planned to host family and friends on Christmas Day. I had mixed feelings about company coming over. I didn't really care if the house was clean or if I had food and gifts for everyone. It just didn't seem that Christmas should happen without Ryan in the house.

As a compromise, I left the house after we opened presents and had our traditional Christmas breakfast. I went to CareMeridian for the rest of the day, and other family and friends visited in shifts. Mama and Daddy came in the early hours, so they could leave to go visit Debby's family. Afterward, they were headed to Hawaii for a two-week vacation.

I poured out my feelings in my journal:

I have confused feelings about that. I know they want to go and Daddy feels he needs a break. Mama needs a good solid time with Daddy. I suppose I need a break from all the time we spend together as well.

What upsets me, though, is how anyone in the family can bear to be away from Ryan. I know I couldn't bear it. I know I'm the only one in this world who can't be torn from his side in order to get a breath and relax for a while. I could not be convinced at this point that it would be good for me. It would break my heart. Ryan is worth every minute I spend with him and every minute I'm away, I'm thinking of him. I know it's because I'm the only one in this world who carried him in my body, nursed him as an infant, and shared his life daily since he was born.

I want everyone to feel as desperate to see him and encourage him, stretch him and love and touch him as I do. I can't imagine feeling any other way toward Ryan. I couldn't let a day go by without personally trying to infuse some of my life and love into him, trying to teach him something new; praying over him while holding his hand or touching his head, trying to motivate him to fight and to work at coming back to us with my hugs and kisses.

I do feel alone because nobody can feel what a mother feels for her child. Not the father, stepfather, grandparents, sister, or brother. They feel what they feel but the connection is not the same. When Jessi has a child, I won't be able to love that child as deeply as she does. I know I have to accept that and forgive when I feel that others have a limit to what they would give—or give up—for Ryan.

There is literally nothing I wouldn't give or give up, but that's me. I'm his mom.

While Mama and Daddy were gone, I got angrier and angrier. I spiraled down into a self-righteous attitude. I felt abandoned in my darkest moment by the people I counted on the most and who had helped me get so far without falling apart. I'd say to myself, *Fine. I'll be the martyr and take care of Ryan by myself since I'm the only one who doesn't seem to feel put out.*

Whenever Daddy called from Hawaii, his cheerful voice was like fingernails on a chalkboard. All I could think was,

I sure hope you're getting a nice, dark tan and improving your golf game. Don't mind us here. I'll take care of Ryan and watch him drool and learn how to change his catheter and his dirty diapers and then figure out what will happen to him in a couple of weeks when he has to leave CareMeridian. But it's more important that you get caught up on your movies and enjoy your house in Hawaii!

I wondered how my mom and dad could bear not seeing Ryan for a couple of weeks. I decided to do both my shift and Mama's shift while she was gone unless another family member happened to show up to give me a break. I decided I wouldn't ask for help because I felt I was now the only one who thought it important to have someone with Ryan at all times. Meanwhile, Mike was looking at new houses as we tried to decide whether to move Ryan into our current house or buy a bigger one.

I finally vented at Mama over the phone. I asked her and Daddy not to call me and act like everything was great, or claim we're "on the verge of a breakthrough" with Ryan. I told them I'd been sick since they left, Jessi was depressed, Mike and I had been arguing about what to do next and where to live, and Ryan wouldn't eat or swallow. On top of it all, I had just been told that I would need to do the unthinkable—learn to change Ryan's diaper and catheter—if I wanted to bring him home. It was unavoidable because if Ryan's caregivers didn't show up for some reason, a trained family member needed to be able to carry out every aspect of his care.

I wrote in my journal:

Ryan is a grown man and I was always planning on having caregivers do the bathing and toileting. We are a modest family and I had a strong reaction to the idea that I would have to cross that line. . . . I felt that if I had to be taught how to do that, I would spiral into a pit I wouldn't be able to crawl out of. How could my parents go on vacation knowing what is going on back home and not want to be here to help?

As I look back, I realize that everyone in my family showed incredible love and self-sacrifice throughout Ryan's recovery. The feelings I experienced were a result of the pressures, my fatigue, and my grief. I was so focused on Ryan and his recovery that I almost didn't see anyone else. Ryan was the center of my world, for better or for worse.

My emotions may also have been going wild because I was no longer on Prozac. While people have to decide for themselves whether or not to use such medications, I had decided I wanted to deal with my pain head-on, and I wasn't able to do that while taking Prozac.

More likely, my feelings of abandonment and martyrdom were triggered when my parents left on their trip, leaving a big hole in my daily routine. Mama and Daddy were my safety net, just as they had always been. They were loving, reliable, and practical, and just about every time I'd had any kind of crisis, as a child or an adult, they had come running to help. But Ryan's accident and his broken, damaged brain were problems my parents couldn't fix. For the first time, I had to stand on my own two feet and figure things out without my parents fixing everything. And now, for the first time since Ryan fell through the skylight, I didn't have my mother to share the highs and the lows, the frustrations and the victories with me. I needed my mother, just as Jessi had needed me.

Yet during that dark time, my family offered me another wave of support. Doug devised a new schedule for family members to take shifts with Ryan. Jessi and I had a deep conversation. I told her that Ryan, in his current condition, was like an infant to me, and I could never leave my baby alone. Until he learned to talk again, or at least communicate somehow, I felt uncomfortable unless I left him with someone I knew and trusted. After our talk, I think Jessi finally understood why it was so important to me that Ryan always have a familiar face, someone who loved him, nearby at all times.

And I had another reason to thank God for my husband. When Mike saw my reaction to having to toilet Ryan, he decided to learn how to do it himself. He didn't discuss it with me in advance, and I had never even considered it an option. But to Mike, it made perfect sense. He was a guy. Guys are used to seeing and hearing all kinds of things in the locker room.

I think if Mike had not stepped up, I would have eventually become accustomed to doing those tasks and survived. But at that time, it felt like more than I could bear, and the relief of not having to take on that part of Ryan's care was greater than I realized. My dear husband learned how to do everything for Ryan, including showering, toileting, and dressing him, and getting him ready for bed.

In my journal I reflected on why this act was so significant to me:

It's not just the extra work that Mike is so willing to take on, but the emotional strength he is showing.

Years before, Mike had taken on a ready-made family when he married me. To do so, he had to first overcome his fears of not being able to relate to Ryan, guy to guy. Over the years, Mike watched Ryan grow into a man, loved him, and didn't hold anything back from him. He took all of our kids on vacation, attended their games and school functions, provided discipline and structure, made them do their chores, gave them guidance, and was generous beyond my expectations. Mike helped put both Ryan and Jessi through college, and we had been looking forward to helping with Ryan's wedding when all of our lives turned upside down.

Cleaning up a toileting accident, putting on a condom catheter, or dressing Ryan must take a huge emotional toll on Mike beyond the time and physical energy he puts into it. This is someone he also loves and it hurts to see his stepson so vulnerable and unable to take care of himself in these simple ways. And to think that Mike was worried about being able to be a good stepdad to Ryan!

Although that Christmas season was the darkest season of my life, and my relationships felt so fragile, shortly after the new year began, I felt as if the emotional roller coaster I was on finally started to climb back up again. My parents returned, our routines started up again, and their love for me absorbed the sharp words I had aimed at them over the phone. Ryan began to improve again too.

And of all things, Larry King wanted us to come back on *Larry King Live* for an update on Ryan. For this third appearance, Larry wanted to visit Ryan in person and see how he was doing. I think he viewed Ryan's recovery as a personal project. And in a way, Larry's show *had* been an important part of Ryan's recovery, prompting prayers around the world to be lifted up to heaven on Ryan's behalf. And the highlight of the show? Well, I don't want to give it away yet. But I'll give you a hint. It involved a well-known restaurant with golden arches.

The show aired January 24, 2002, and Larry opened the show by posing a dramatic question: Did the power of prayer lead to Ryan's miraculous recovery? Video footage ran of Ryan, looking more awake and alert, shaking hands with Larry using the secret Sigma Nu handshake my dad had shown him. Also on the show with Daddy and me were my sister Debby, Dave Owen, and Kenneth Copeland.

Larry did a recap of Ryan's accident and the long period he was in a coma. He explained that the doctors had offered little hope that Ryan would ever get off the ventilator and that we'd even been advised to withdraw life support early on.

"Did you ever give up faith?" Larry asked me.

"Oh, no. He is my son. . . . My hope is in the Lord," I answered.

Before airing more footage of his visit to Ryan at CareMeridian, Larry turned to the camera and said, "I was there and it's remarkable." Daddy had ridden with Larry in the back of the limo to visit Ryan, while I took a separate car. Daddy told me later that, off camera in the car, he asked Larry about his faith and why he didn't have the answers he'd been searching for.

Larry told my dad how the loss of his own father had devastated him. His parents were Russian immigrants who were observant Jews and kept a kosher home. Every Shabbat, his mother would light the candles, and the family celebrated all the holidays. Then one day when Larry was nine years old, his father dropped dead at the plant where he worked, leaving Larry's mother to raise two boys on her own.

My dad recalls Larry saying, "You believe God is all powerful, all knowing, all loving. Why does he let terrible things happen to good people? I had Rabbi Kushner [the author of *Why Bad Things Happen to Good People*] on to try to explain, but no one ever gave a satisfactory answer. Why would God let that happen to my dad?"

Now we were beginning to understand a little better why Larry seemed so interested in Ryan and in how we were responding to our own personal tragedy. Larry had us under a microscope.

Larry seemed happy to meet Ryan and watched as Ryan gave us kisses. Daddy talked about how we were eagerly awaiting the chance to hear Ryan's voice again. "I hope his first word is *Mom*," Daddy said.

Back in the studio, Debby talked about the effects of the accident on me. "I have seen a strength. . . . It has changed my life watching what God has done in my sister [as she went through] something that's unimaginable as a mother." Debby went on to say that when bad things do happen, people naturally look to God. It's okay to have doubts, she said: "Doubt helps your faith increase. Don't be afraid of your doubts. Address them, look at them, and find out what's true."

Larry had one last question for me. It was a hard one. "Lindy, you don't say, 'Why me?'"

"No, that doesn't cross my mind because everywhere you look there are troubles," I said, thinking of the many trials of the last few months. Then I quoted a lifeline verse that I had been holding on to: "Jesus said, 'I have told you these things, so that in Me you may have [perfect] peace and confidence. In the world you have tribulation and trials and distress and frustration; but be of good cheer [take courage; be confident, certain, undaunted]! For I have overcome the world'" (John 16:33, AMP).

Daddy talked about God's love for us, which Jesus demonstrated on the cross, and that was followed by an old clip of Daddy singing "Jesus Loves Me" with three-year-old Ryan.

Probably one of the most powerful video clips that evening was of Ryan's outing to McDonald's. In preparation for Ryan's move home, we'd bought a wheelchair van so we could transport him to appointments and therapy. Ryan's speech therapist, who was also working with Ryan on his eating, suggested we take Ryan on an outing to see how he'd do. She suggested McDonald's, since the environment would be familiar to him and she thought he might be motivated to try eating their food.

It was a triumphant moment for a young man who had lost so much, who was just learning to eat again, and who had not been outside the hospital except when being transported to another hospital. On Ryan's visit to McDonald's, he sat in his wheelchair and ate part of a burger, fries, and a few sips of a shake with our help. While we'd been offering him food regularly before this, sometimes he had been able to eat only one bite before stopping. On many days, chewing and swallowing simply took more energy than he had. That's why we were so excited to see him eat a number of bites at McDonald's. He ate more at this meal than he had at any other since his accident.

Most other diners at McDonald's weren't paying much attention to our group, but we were so excited. I turned to a woman at another table who was watching her own child play and proclaimed, "You're watching a miracle."

It was the happiest Happy Meal of all.

Here are a few e-mails from Larry's viewers after our third appearance:

Please embrace Ryan and tell him that there is this lady from Prince Edward Island, about five thousand miles from where he is living, and that she's praying each and every day, holding him up to Jesus. . . . Embrace your son with love daily and feel alive, knowing that he is with you. Jesus lives within Ryan. This is exciting.

✦

What a strong man Ryan is. I am so touched by his strength and it gives me my own personal strength in my hard time. Thanks to Ryan, I do not wish I was dead anymore. . . . I know that God has made me for a reason and I hope to live my life the best I can, just like Ryan.

✦

I do believe, as you all do, that the reasons for Ryan's accident are immense and profound.

✦

We know Ryan has a burden to reach his generation for Christ and we will pray God will use him to do this. I am sure in many ways he already has.

✦

Ryan, you are a true testimony to the power of God and I pray for the day that you, yourself, are on Larry King Live, *because I know it is going to happen.*

✦ ✦ ✦

Over the next month, Ryan started to mouth words. He didn't have any strength in his voice but we could see him respond to things we said with a single word or short phrase. We started to see him mouth words like *Mom, okay, bye,* and even *I love you.* It was exciting, but oddly, he still didn't show any facial expression.

The next thing we discovered was that Ryan could read! His therapist found out while showing him single words on a flash card. Sure enough, Ryan could mouth whatever little word or short phrase he saw. That told us so much—he could see and he could read.

It had been a long, slow process, but it was official. Ryan was no longer in a coma. Early in 2002 we moved Ryan yet again. This time he moved to Long Beach Memorial Medical Center, an hour's drive from my house, so we could try hyperbaric oxygen therapy to promote healing of the damaged cells in Ryan's brain. It was an expensive therapy that involved placing Ryan in an airtight, pressurized chamber that resembled a tanning bed. Because the pressure inside is similar to that undersea, it forces more oxygen into the cells. It seems to help some people with brain injury but not others.

It's best done every day and as soon as possible after the initial injury. Ryan's treatment plan called for ninety minutes a day for five weeks. We soon encountered a problem, however. Few people at this facility had been trained to do a simple transfer of a patient, such as moving Ryan from his bed to a wheelchair or commode chair. At other facilities, we had gotten used to having a trained staff member available who could move Ryan to a sitting position on the edge of his bed, lift him, then pivot him to a chair next to the bed. In Long Beach, however, the nurses used a Hoyer Lift, a heavy metal apparatus on wheels. Ryan had to be rolled over onto his side and then a canvas or fabric sling was placed underneath him. The sling was attached to metal bars that were then raised high enough to lift his body off the bed and into a chair.

It usually took two or three nurses to figure out how to get this six-foot-four man, all legs and arms, moved from bed to chair. Every time I had to watch this awkward and time-consuming process, I wanted to fade away and retreat from life.

An awful moment occurred one day when the nurses had finally lifted Ryan from his bed and seated him on a portable toilet seat in a safety frame, which would then be wheeled over the toilet so Ryan could have a bowel movement. Right then, a nurse came in to give him some medication through his feeding tube. She assured us it would take just a moment. But as she was giving him the meds, I realized Ryan was about to empty his bowels. Right there. On the floor of his room in front of his mother and three women he didn't know at all.

Afterward, I comforted him. "It's all right, Ryan. It's not your fault." I told him it was no problem cleaning it up. He showed no expression and had no way of communicating any embarrassment. I could only wonder what was going on in his mind. *Is he aware that he was defecating uncontrollably in front of people he doesn't know? Does he feel the inappropriateness of the situation? Is he trying to control it? Is he humiliated?*

I had no way of knowing. But it was excruciatingly painful for me to witness. When the ladies wheeled his commode chair over the toilet, I excused myself, as I always did, to give my son privacy. I walked through the door to the hall and fell against the wall, holding my face. As my legs weakened, I slowly lowered myself to the floor and cried, not caring who was around to see me. I hated this. I hated the Hoyer Lift and how it made Ryan look like a sack of potatoes instead of a man.

During this time, Ryan's tendons and ligaments began to get tighter and his legs drew together. Motion therapy was important but it wasn't enough; Ryan's spasticity was getting worse. One of the doctors noticed and volunteered to do surgery.

"I could cut his tendons for you. I'm a surgeon and I've done that many times for people like your son."

I knew he was trying to help, but I didn't like the sound of that at all. I didn't want to seem stupid, but I had to ask. "If you did that, would that mean Ryan wouldn't be able to walk?"

I could see the disbelief on his face as he realized that I still thought walking was going to be in Ryan's future. "Well, yes, if I cut his tendons he would never walk again. But he would be much more comfortable."

"I'm still planning on seeing Ryan walk again. So, no. Thank you."

I tried to be kind in my response, but I was a little angry at his implication. He had already decided that my son was never going to walk again so the best option was to make him as comfortable as possible.

We ended up with a much better solution using baclofen, a muscle relaxant. While he was at Long Beach Memorial, a baclofen pump was surgically placed in Ryan's abdomen with a catheter that ran from the pump directly into his spinal column. As the baclofen was released into his spinal fluid, it helped relax his muscles and tendons. When the medication was used up, a light alarm would sound and a doctor would be able to refill the pump by inserting a syringe into a port on the pump, accessible through the skin of Ryan's belly.

The procedure worked. Ryan's legs loosened up, although his left arm remained tight. And joy of joys, I saw Ryan's first smile just a day or two before he was released to come home with us. It had been ten months since his accident. On that morning, I walked into the ICU, where he was recovering after having the pump put in. The moment I did, a smile started to form and build on Ryan's face. It startled me, and I looked around. I was the only one there!

I stuck my head out the door of the room, already weeping with joy, and called to a nurse. "Come quick!"

I realized she thought it was an emergency, so I quickly added, "It's a good thing. I need a witness."

The nurse hurried over and saw Ryan's smile just as it was starting to fade. What a milestone. And I knew one thing for sure: if I saw it once, I would see it again.

That was the pattern I had learned. Ryan would do something new and sometimes I would get frustrated because it might not happen again for a while. But if he did it once, it would happen again. There would be more smiles. More words. More Happy Meals.

And some day, I just knew he would walk.

✦　✦　✦

As Ryan was completing his hyperbaric oxygen treatments at Long Beach Memorial, we were busy making modifications to our home so that Ryan could move in with us. We had decided to remain there, though doing so required Mike to take on a number of remodeling projects. In addition to installing two wheelchair ramps leading up to the house, we converted our downstairs guest room into Ryan's room, expanding the adjoining bathroom so a prefabricated handicap-accessible shower could be added. Finally we converted part of our garage into a small physical therapy room.

While Mike finished our home makeover, I began looking for caregivers to take on what I considered the most important job in the world—taking care of my son. From the day we first began discussing bringing Ryan home, I began praying that the Lord would provide exactly the right people to help us: *Lord, you have brought us this far. Now I have to ask you another favor.* I had to trust his caregivers to watch over Ryan as he slept and to help with every part of his care. I wanted them to know and really care about Ryan. Because I knew I wasn't aware of everything that should be considered, I knew I needed God to handle this for me.

Then I met James. He was the one member of the Long Beach Memorial staff who could do a proper transfer for my son. He was a certified nurse's assistant, and every time he came in on his shift, I felt lighter. He was warm and friendly and would chat about this or that with me while he was caring for Ryan. And he didn't need any stinkin' Hoyer Lift!

Besides James, we also met Joseph, a certified nurse's assistant my parents hired to be with Ryan from 10 p.m. to 7 a.m. each day. I knew the hospital staff would leave Ryan completely alone at times during the night, and I still felt someone needed to be with him in case he needed help. Joseph had a warm smile and was smart and articulate, taking perfect notes through each night.

Though Ryan's insurance covered twenty-four-hour-a-day nursing care for the first several weeks he was home, James and Joseph helped take care of Ryan from the first day he moved home with us from the hospital. These two angels from heaven are more than caregivers and employees; they have become beloved members of the family.

Because I knew insurance would pay for only six hours of in-home therapy (physical, occupational, and speech) each week, I also made a point to visit a nonprofit brain injury program in Tustin, California, that I'd heard about called High Hopes. I thought it might fill in some of the gaps insurance didn't cover. High Hopes' director, Mark Desmond, took me on a tour of the facility. As excited as I was to see the equipment and staff available to work with Ryan, it was difficult to watch the students, many of whom seemed largely unresponsive. Mark told me that High Hopes accepted people with all degrees of brain injury and would work with them in any way that would help them progress.

We agreed that Ryan would start slowly, attending High Hopes twice a week for a couple of hours at a time. The sadness I'd felt during my tour quickly gave way to renewed hope and optimism. The staff was so warm and helpful that I felt my spirits lift whenever I hung out there. To show me what was possible for Ryan, they told me stories of the great recoveries some of the students had made. Mark was very hands-on, and I loved finding out more about what the staff did there and why, and what I could be doing at home with Ryan to support their efforts.

✦ ✦ ✦

Eight months after millions of viewers around the world saw Ryan eating at McDonald's, we were invited back to *Larry King Live* to give an update. Finally we had plenty of good news to report to his audience. Not only was Ryan now back home, he was relearning speech and movement. He could eat and drink, and his voice was beginning to return, although it was still breathy. He was also learning how to focus his attention; sometimes he seemed to mentally check out and go into a fog and we'd try hard to engage him and bring him out of it.

Joining Daddy and me for our fourth appearance on Larry's show were Dr. Robert Schuller of the Crystal Cathedral near Los Angeles, Dr. Jack Hayford of The Church on the Way in Van Nuys (my parents' church), Jessi, and my sister Debby.

Larry wanted to highlight Ryan's progress and showed video clips of Daddy singing to Ryan, and Ryan mouthing the words along with Daddy; Ryan reading flash cards; and Ryan and me talking, with Ryan responding and rubbing my arm. One powerful clip showed Ryan whispering to us, his voice still breathy, "Good morning" and "I love you."

Jessi talked to Larry about how Ryan's accident had impacted her faith and about her strong bond with her older brother. "I get so much love from him," she said. "He's full of love." We told Larry what a blessing it was to have Ryan home, and how God had answered those prayers that had started from the first instant we heard of the accident. But we still needed more prayer for Ryan's restoration.

On this show, as he had done on the others, Daddy talked about his faith in Christ. Larry gave him an open forum and he shared, fearlessly, the gospel of the Lord Jesus.

Debby closed out the show singing "You Light Up My Life," those oh-so-familiar lyrics about faith, hope, and dreams infused with an extra measure of meaning for all of us who were part of this ongoing demonstration of God's faithfulness and mercy. We were all hoping that someday Ryan would come on Larry's show himself. With the demands of live television and the complicated logistics of getting him to the studio and keeping him comfortable, it would be difficult. But I believed it would happen.

Here are e-mails from Larry's viewers:

This is just to let you know that another person is praying for Ryan. There is no doubt that God has great plans for him and he knows what they are.

✦

I was deeply touched by your will to survive. Though you have not recovered fully physically, what is important is YOU, who [are more than] this body. . . . We have a song in our language which says, even if gold has a defect, the glory of gold is not dulled. If a lion's leg is injured, his bravery doesn't diminish.

✦

Dear Pat: I watched you, Larry King, Lindy, and the panel on CNN. I must say that I think that hour did more for helping people to understand God and prayer than all of the church services I've seen, combined.

✦

Something about Ryan has stayed with me and touched my soul. . . . I have not been able to think of anything else.

✦

I was deeply touched by Ryan's story—so much that I cancelled the appointment I had to have my cable discontinued. I want to see Ryan when he comes on Larry King.

✦

Ryan, you will be a great witness for the entire world to see. Just hang in there. Let God's love make you whole.

CHAPTER 12

DON'T READ THIS IF YOU'RE EASILY OFFENDED

Words written fifty years ago, a hundred years ago,
a thousand years ago, can have as much of this power today
as ever they had it then to come alive for us and in us
and to make us more alive within ourselves.

FREDERICK BUECHNER

FOR THE FIRST TWO YEARS following Ryan's accident, I struggled with fatigue, conflict, and depression. Then in the fall of 2003, a whole new struggle came along that brought some of the greatest stress to me personally.

With Ryan's increasing mental awareness and improved cognition came an issue we hadn't expected at this stage of Ryan's recovery—one we are still dealing with. Ryan's core personality had always been warm, loving, and empathetic. His sister used to joke that she was more of a man than he was. (You've gotta love baby sisters and their teasing, right?) So when this problem began to manifest, I was completely shocked.

Looking back, I realize that it began to develop about a year and a half after the accident, when Ryan started to show signs of being startled when any adult male approached him. This was particularly obvious at church. He wasn't speaking much then, but people would greet him lovingly. "We're so happy to see you!" they'd exclaim. For the first several weeks, Ryan would smile and seem happy too.

Gradually, however, we began to notice him getting overly excited and yelling (mouth and eyes wide open, but little voice yet) whenever a man would approach him to say hello or shake his hand. This happened only with men, not women. Since he wasn't talking much yet, I didn't quite know how to read his odd reaction. Most people didn't seem bothered by it, so I would tell them he was just excited. It was becoming difficult to be in public but we loved taking him out to be around people.

About two years into Ryan's recovery, the yelling turned into four-letter words. I finally realized he wasn't just excited, he was extremely upset. The words became more and more frequent, loud, and aggressive. Not only that, but Ryan began using his right arm to try to strike out at any man who approached him. He would also spit to drive the person away. This behavior was directed even to his own father and to Daddy Pat. These two men loved him dearly and visited often but felt so confused. I was heartbroken and perplexed. *How can Ryan not want to be near them? Should we force the issue or let his behavior drive them away?*

There is a certain irony to the situation. Through the years as I've prayed for Ryan, put my own faith and beliefs into words, and experienced the healing power of others' words, I've learned to better choose what I say. I guard my words and have grown more sensitive to how others use them too.

I have never been one to use four-letter words. I just don't cuss. I have my faults, but thanks to Mama and Daddy, I was raised not to swear. I don't mind being around people who cuss if it's not superexcessive; I realize it can be just a habit, a by-product of the environment a person grew up in. In fact, my own husband has a colorful way of speaking. Because I knew he wasn't raised the same way I was and didn't profess to follow Christ when we were dating, it didn't really bother me. Becoming a Christian doesn't immediately take those words out of your vocabulary, although I have noticed that, slowly but surely, Mike is also becoming more aware of the power of his words.

In any event, I've had to grow a much thicker skin. Doctors have theorized that something in Ryan's damaged brain sees males as a threat, which sets off a fear reaction whenever one approaches. This perceived threat leads to a fight-or-flight situation in his mind, so his nervous system pumps adrenaline and other chemicals through his body to bring him to a state of heightened alert, almost as if he's facing a life-threatening emergency. And it's beyond his control.

The confusing part of all this is that, while Ryan's brain might be misfiring as he yells, "F--- you; I don't like you" (which became the most repetitive phrase in his repertoire), the reality is he has no intention of hurting anyone. The irony is that Ryan always loved people and used words wisely and effectively. That was the real Ryan, and I believe that, apart from the injury, it still is.

As soon as these outbursts subside, Ryan says, "I'm sorry." We've talked about it, and he has no idea why this happens. Because of that, I've learned that although words themselves have power, the intention behind those words adds to their strength. In Ryan's case, there is no intention to say those words, any more than people with Tourette's syndrome intend to repeat their tics. Anyone who spends much time with Ryan has had to learn how to let those words bounce off and roll away. They can't let them penetrate their heart because they are not meant to.

That's easier said than done, however. So every day, I hear more profanity than a member of the Osborne family. I'm used to it now, but it wasn't always easy. When I first got caught in the cross fire, it felt like stab wounds to my heart when Ryan hit me, bit me, or called me a b----.

I've wept an ocean of tears over this situation. Not only has it hurt me to see Ryan go through this, but it has restricted our activities with him in public and distracted him in therapy.

Early on, I was on the phone with Ryan's doctor often. He prescribed a number of different medications but nothing worked. Some meds made him sleepy, but that impaired any cognitive progress we were trying to make. Other medications did nothing at all. Finally, I took Ryan to see the doctor so he could witness the behavior. During our visit, Ryan conducted a violent tirade for twenty minutes without a break. The doctor agreed it was more serious than he had imagined. He suggested Ryan live in a facility that could not only give him therapy but also address this very difficult behavioral issue. Everyone he came in contact with at such a residential facility would know how to respond to his behavior appropriately. That was the only hope of extinguishing it.

However, there were no such facilities nearby, and I knew if Ryan had to go live somewhere else, I would have to live near him. I didn't want him to feel abandoned. I could not drop him off somewhere and just check in on him now and again. If he woke up in a new place with no familiar faces, he wouldn't remember where he was or who the caretakers were. Though he recognized his friends and family and remembered much of his life before the accident, his short-term memory was still poor. For example, when he watched a movie, he forgot what he'd watched almost immediately afterward. And this from a guy who had always loved movies and could remember the names of obscure character actors!

After looking at several facilities, we moved Ryan to the Centre for Neuro Skills (CNS) in Bakersfield, California, which offered neurobehavioral therapy. I had no idea how long Ryan or I would be there, so the move stirred up unanswerable questions. Jessi had moved back to San Francisco by this point, so I wasn't worried about her. But Tyler would be turning seventeen soon and needed his parents; some of his behavior was beginning to concern Mike and me. I knew it was a bad time to be away from him, and I agonized about not being able to be two places at once.

Mike knew I had to be with Ryan, but he hoped I'd get comfortable enough with the facility to trust them with Ryan. Mama came to the rescue again and helped me find a two-bedroom condo down the road from the CNS apartment building where Ryan would be living. I was so relieved she would be there with me; I didn't know a soul in Bakersfield.

Caregivers employed by CNS transported Ryan to the clinic every day for six hours of therapy, and he made many gains during his year there. He became more verbal overall, his cognition improved, and more movement became possible. He could lean forward with improved trunk strength, and he learned to bridge, or lift his hips off the floor when his knees were bent, which helped his caregivers when they were dressing him.

During Ryan's time at CNS, I divided my time between Bakersfield and home. Mike was impatient with me gone so much; he felt a crisis building with our younger son. When I was gone, Mike argued often with Tyler, who was becoming increasingly sullen and rebellious. I reasoned that Tyler had his dad, our home, his school, his friends, and his golf team. He knew where I was and I called, wrote letters, and began coming home on weekends, leaving Mama to keep Ryan company.

Ryan had nothing familiar except Mama and me. And Ryan needed something the caregivers absolutely couldn't give. He needed love. If I wasn't there, who would love him? Who would hug him and give him kisses? Who would talk to him about his life and tell him he was doing well but needed to try harder? Who would pray with him at night and speak life and recovery over his body and brain? My mother and me. We had to be there.

As the year went on, I sensed more and more judgment from members of my family. Some of them questioned why I spent so much time in Bakersfield. They were sure Ryan would be just fine whether or not I was with him so much. Looking back, it's much easier to see from their perspective, but I still don't think I'd have done anything else. I drove to Bakersfield every Monday at 5 a.m. to beat traffic, arriving by 8 a.m. I'd spend the week with Ryan, then leave at 9 p.m. Friday to arrive back home by midnight and spend the weekend with Mike and Tyler. I thought it worked well, given the circumstances. I also knew it was temporary.

I tried to concentrate on my family on the weekends,

filling Saturdays and Sundays with fun, friends, and family. I also worked hard to bond with Tyler when I was home, but it was tough; he was testing boundaries and often Mike and I would have to deal with rules, consequences, and attitudes. Plus, Tyler really didn't want to hang out with us all that much. (Although, to be fair, it's not uncommon for teenage boys not to be interested in hanging out with their parents.)

As Tyler continued acting out, Jessi, my cheerleader, my bright spot, began to speak up. She was worried about Tyler and frightened about what was happening. When I'd want to tell her about some new thing Ryan accomplished or something funny he said, she didn't want to hear it. At this point, I felt like it was me against the world. My mom was there, God bless her, but I just felt like I couldn't please anyone in my immediate family.

My life, for twenty-six years, had revolved around being a mother. My three children were the center of my life. When Ryan fell, he took front and center. Now the rest of my family was falling apart, and they thought I didn't care. But I did. I knew my husband wanted me home because he loved and missed me. Jessi wanted me home because she was worried about Tyler; she didn't want to lose *two* brothers. She worried that if I didn't do something, the family might not survive. She often said I held the key to everything. The pressure was intense.

I realize now that every single person in our family suffered deep wounds from Ryan's accident. He's not the only one who fell through the skylight. We all crashed through to a very different life from the happy, problem-free existence we'd enjoyed before. Each one of us was damaged. There were no fatalities, thank God. But, eventually, as Ryan recovered, I realized the other members of my family needed to be tended to. They had looked out for me after the accident, but Mike, Jessi, and Tyler, who had waited so patiently, now needed my attention.

Family counseling, which we were able to fit in at the start of a few weekends, helped some. I don't think there was any perfect solution; our circumstances were extraordinary. But we all endured that year and when it ended, much of the stress was relieved. We still had to deal with the ways Tyler was acting out, but Mike and I were able to rely on God and have seen great growth and maturity develop in our younger son, who is now a man. I have no doubt that his anger and acting out had much to do with the trauma he experienced as a thirteen-year-old when his brother nearly died.

Jessi has forgiven me for the ways I let her down too. I know I haven't been the best mother to her and to Tyler. Had Ryan's accident never happened, things might have been different. But God knows—and I hope Jessi and Tyler both know—how precious they are to me. I would pour out my life and energy for any of my children.

Ryan came back home after a year. Even though he'd made gains, his stay had taken a toll on us in every way. One bright spot during this time was that God sent another angel caregiver: Chris, who now worked with Ryan on Saturdays and Sundays. There was something in his quiet way that Ryan responded to. He was lean but strong and he really seemed to like Ryan, despite the unique challenges of his behavior. They were both huge sports fans. Chris began to work for us, joining us as a third caregiver at home.

While we saw improvement in Ryan's angry behavior while at CNS, it was inconsistent. We had discovered that if Ryan was in the same environment or with the same people every day, the sense of danger passed and his outbursts diminished. Yet when he was in public or unfamiliar situations, I could see him struggle to fight the instinct to lash out that came from an overstimulated part of his brain. So we still felt stuck.

Then we discovered Ativan (lorazepam), an anti-anxiety medication that works by slowing activity in the brain to allow for relaxation. Ativan was wonderful—it calmed Ryan so he behaved normally, and it even helped improve his speech.

I knew it would be a challenge for Ryan to see the dentist for the first time since his accident, but on Ativan, he cooperated with the dentist with no cussing or hitting. He even calmly looked at me and said, "Getting your teeth cleaned is a healthy process." I was delighted that he put such a long sentence together and said it clearly, and it made sense! But my elation at the successful dentist visit was soon deflated when we realized Ativan can't be used every day without causing dependency because the body builds up a tolerance to it. We decided to use Ativan only when most needed.

In fact, while Ativan worked for a while, its effectiveness began to diminish. Ambien, which is most commonly prescribed to treat insomnia, also calms the brain and has been somewhat effective for about ninety minutes at a time. Initially we used it every day so Ryan could work through therapy at High Hopes without the distracting outbursts. Now that Ryan has become adjusted to the environment at High Hopes, he no longer needs to take it daily. The medication also works well for a meal at a restaurant or for a doctor's appointment. If necessary, we're able to give Ryan Ambien every day—even twice a day—and it gives us three hours of controlled, appropriate behavior, for the most part.

We've had our awkward moments, though. One day we decided to go to SeaWorld with Ryan. As we got close to the park, I could see the landmark steel tower and knew we were almost there. Ryan's caregiver had given him the right dose of Ativan at just the right time so it would take full effect by the time we got to the park. I was excited and really looking forward to a fun day of watching all the shows with Ryan.

I was in the far right lane with my eyes trained on the SeaWorld tower when I realized I was in a right-turn-only lane. I didn't know the area that well and it looked safe for me to go straight, so rather than turning and getting lost, I broke the law and drove straight. When I saw a police car pull right in behind me, I knew I'd been caught red-handed and deserved whatever I got.

I rolled the window down as the officer stepped up to the car and all of a sudden, Ryan did his thing. He *loudly* let the police officer know he had come too close and wasn't welcome. Apparently his medication hadn't kicked in yet. Over the string of expletives directed at the officer, I explained apologetically that my son had a brain injury that caused him to say these things. I told the police officer it wasn't intentional and he didn't mean what he was saying.

The officer looked at me. "Good luck," he said sincerely, and walked away without giving me a ticket. I was so relieved! I hope you aren't offended when I tell you about all the high-fiving we did in the car as we drove away. When I've told that story to friends and family, don't think it hasn't crossed their minds to use a similar tactic the next time they get pulled over.

CHAPTER 13

RYAN'S REACH

All I know is that all my life, I never walked 'cause my legs never grew the way they were supposed to. But then this young fella comes over to my street, talking about God and all this other stuff, and before I know it, my legs started to grow! I can't explain it, ma'am. I can only thank God for it every day.

DURING THE FIRST few months after Ryan's accident, I didn't think much about all the medical costs or wonder how we were going to pay for them. My daily concerns were for Ryan's condition. I relied on Mike and Doug to figure out the financial stuff. I assumed there was insurance in place to cover what would be needed. I also assumed we would do whatever needed to be done to make sure his care and therapy were paid for.

I admit that, coming from an affluent family, I'd never had to worry much about the basic necessities of life. I went through separations and a divorce. I lived as a single mom with two children, and I did have some very lean times where I counted my pennies as I tried to make ends meet. But the reality is I was blessed to have alimony, child support, and ultimately my parents as a safety net. I always knew I could reach out to them for help. And when Ryan fell, I knew they would always be there for him, and for me.

At some point, however, insurance coverage would run out. And it became clear to all of us that we needed to be thinking about Ryan's care and recovery in terms of decades. Ryan was just in his twenties and would probably need care and therapy for many years. He was recovering, but progress was slow.

My family and I have always prayed with an expectation that Ryan will be restored. "He will live and not die and declare the glory of God" was and is our verse for Ryan. So how would we reconcile having strong faith in God's will to heal Ryan while also planning for a future with a disabled son? The only thing that made sense was to stay surrendered to whatever God had in store for Ryan, regardless of the outcome. I wanted to remain humble, not test the Lord, and always hope for the best. I also felt my role was to speak life, health, and recovery into his life. I worked hard to live every day with gratitude for Ryan's life and his recovery up to that point, but I continued to speak more and to believe more was on the way.

Meanwhile, Mike and Doug sheltered me from the huge concerns about how we would cope if the insurance company denied Ryan care, an ever-present possibility. As Ryan emerged from the coma and began to recover, I slowly became more aware of the financial issues and I became very grateful that I was married to a lawyer. Within the first week of the accident, Mike had the presence of mind and the training to know that he needed to visit the building where Ryan fell. I couldn't bear to go with him, but Doug went.

At the Dorothy Street apartment building, Mike and

Doug took photos of the roof (the door was still unlocked), the skylight, the walkways (with the dents from Ryan's body still there), and the floor where he landed. Then Mike hired an investigator to research building codes, and he slowly started to prepare a case for liability on the part of the building owners. Mike always does his homework and is a detail-oriented guy. I think he's that way naturally, but years of legal training and experience honed his instincts and he knew what evidence would be needed for court. He started communicating with the landlord's insurance company owners about the possibility of a settlement to avoid going to court. But Mike knew, after conducting research and talking to experts, that the insurance payment would not be sufficient to provide for Ryan's care for the rest of his life.

Mike wrote to the insurance company and asked if they planned to pay the full coverage amount. After many letters and e-mails were exchanged, it became clear the insurance company was going to offer a lesser settlement than the policy limit. They must have believed they could save themselves some money, but their response amazed Mike.

That's because he knew their failure to offer the designated policy limit was exposing the owner of the building to personal liability for a judgment exceeding the policy limit. In other words, because the insurance company refused to pay out the full amount, they weren't doing their job of protecting the apartment building owners. In legal terms, this is called "bad faith." When I asked Mike to explain, he said the building owner would have a case of its own against the insurance company for having acted in bad faith by not tendering the full amount of the coverage limit. Now the insurance company would be facing two teams of attorneys, one team representing Ryan, and the other, the building owners. The legal profession refers to this scenario as the insurance company's having "opened up the policy." In short, the written policy limit was no longer the maximum exposure to the insurance company. Rather, they could now be held liable for an entire judgment set by a jury.

You can now see why I was so happy to leave this in Mike's hands. But I think it's important to give you an overview of the financial and legal issues in case you or someone you love is ever forced to deal with something similar. When a traumatic accident occurs, survival and recovery are the priority. But at some point, these other issues have to be handled too.

At this stage in the process, Mike decided to retain an attorney more experienced in this kind of legal case and found one in the widely respected Wylie Aitken. Eventually, all parties sat across a table from one another, and a settlement far in excess of the policy limit was reached. Ryan's case had a high profile, his injuries were enormous, and the expected cost of care over many years was extremely high. Mike wondered how the insurance company could not have understood and complied with the most basic principle of insurance coverage: offer the policy limit if it will protect the insured from a personal judgment.

The insurance settlement enabled us to set Ryan up with a monthly annuity that covers the many expenses of caring for him and continuing rehabilitation, rather than just maintaining the status quo. Our family is able to have a life alongside Ryan, assisted by caregivers. As Ryan continues to recover, he needs someone to be with him at all times and assist him in just about everything. He has many doctor's appointments and therapies, none of which are inexpensive, and there have been many trips to the emergency room for infections or seizures. Mike considered the outcome a true miracle, another intervention from the Lord.

However, I know we are in the vast minority. I meet so many people who have lost everything and whose lives are consumed with personally caring for a loved one who has suffered a traumatic injury. I understand that my life is much easier because of the settlement Ryan received. I also know that while I suffered so much emotional pain over what happened to Ryan, I was protected from much of the financial worry. Ryan needed this settlement; it was not some slick maneuver that resulted in an unfair deal. But still, my life would be very different today if we'd been limited to the amount the insurance company offered in the early stages.

And that's a big reason I feel obligated to put my energy, creativity, and prayers toward helping those who don't have the resources Ryan does. As a family, we created a foundation to help people with traumatic brain injuries get the care they need. The opportunity to be a blessing to others has been bought, in a way, by this amazing insurance settlement.

The idea for the foundation began, for me, when a friend started introducing Ryan to celebrities. This friend was a frequent visitor to the hospital during those early months, and when Ryan came home, she started looking for other ways to help. She'd come and read to him so I could take a break and go out for a bit, or she'd bring over some homemade barbecued beef that Ryan loved. As Ryan improved even more, she started contacting various celebrities whom she thought

Ryan might like to meet in person or have a signed memento from. Much to our surprise, several well-known celebrities and athletes responded, and we were able to take Ryan on some outings to meet some of the people he admired in the entertainment business. Ryan wasn't yet able to carry on a conversation, but you could see in his eyes that he knew whom he was meeting. We felt we were helping to bring some new, pleasurable experiences into his life.

So between our appearances on Larry King and the celebrities who showed openhearted willingness to meet Ryan, we began to see a larger picture. Was it possible to take the platform we'd been offered and see if we could use it for even more good? Could we raise awareness of traumatic brain injury? Would it be possible to help other families who needed information, resources, and even financial assistance? As a family, we decided to take the plunge and start a foundation in Ryan's name to raise money for others in our situation.

As I thought about the foundation one morning, I prayed for just the right name. "Ryan's Reach" popped into my head. In my mind, I could see Ryan with one hand reaching out to God, his family, and the medical community for his own recovery. But I could also see him reaching with his other hand to bring as many people as possible along the road to recovery with him. We formed a board of directors, with Doug as chair, and we all agreed on the name, Ryan's Reach. The foundation was officially launched in April 2003.

Daddy has been an important part of the foundation's success. I'm not sure it would exist without him. As a beloved entertainer with over fifty years in the music industry, he's sown seeds of blessing into our culture and numerous worthy charities and causes over the decades. Because of his fan base and his well-known Christian testimony, he's earned love and respect in Hollywood and throughout the world. I am thankful for his long-standing reputation; because of his fame, he brought attention to Ryan's accident. His friendship with Larry King resulted in the appearances that started people praying from around the world, and it's my dad's recognizable name that allows us to hold an annual Pat Boone and Friends Golf Classic to benefit Ryan's Reach. Celebrity golfers have included Robert Hays, John Ratzenberger, John O'Hurley, Chris Knight, and Al Joyner.

Another yearly fund-raiser is the Dove Dash, a 5K and 10K walk/race with a community pancake breakfast and raffle. We release forty white doves that fly out over the crowd, and then a cannon booms to start the race. Daddy is the emcee and makes good use of a bullhorn to urge participants on. At the end of the race, Ryan stands up out of his wheelchair, and Mike, Tyler, Doug, and Ryan cross the finish line together. Every year, I cry when I see it.

As we raised money through these fund-raisers, we had to decide specifically what to do with the proceeds. The numbers are mind boggling. Over 1.7 million people sustain a traumatic brain injury (TBI) in the United States every year.[22] According to the Centers for Disease Control and Injury Prevention, the leading cause of traumatic brain injury is a fall (35 percent).[23] Other common causes include motor vehicle–traffic crashes, accidental blows to the head, and assaults. Blasts are the leading cause of TBI for military personnel in war zones.[24]

The cost of care for these millions of people is astronomical. One of the problems is that no two brain injuries are exactly the same. The effects of a brain injury are complex and vary greatly from person to person, depending on the cause, location, and severity.[25] There is no standard, straightforward treatment or therapy that works in every case. Care is individualized and must constantly be adjusted.

We pledged Ryan's Reach to become a supporting foundation to High Hopes, the injury program Ryan attends for people with head injuries. The money we raised would go toward helping their students. We reasoned that if we could afford to buy a piece of equipment from donations, it made sense to put that equipment where dozens of people could use it, rather than give it to a single household where only one person could use it.

We also realized we could fund scholarships for people who needed therapy but couldn't afford the monthly fee to attend High Hopes, and we are grateful to know that people are making gains in their recovery because of those scholarships. Our ultimate vision is to grow big enough to help High Hopes reproduce. One High Hopes is great, but multiple High Hopes facilities would help so many more people. Overall, it's estimated that at least 5.3 million Americans with TBI currently have a long-term need for help to perform activities of daily living.[26] The need is great.

Although there are many good facilities around the country that are equipped to work with and help someone recover from a head injury, unless the injured person is wealthy, once the insurance limit is reached, that can be the end of access to a rehabilitation facility. I remember the time I heard that

Ryan wasn't progressing quickly enough to remain in a particular hospital rehabilitation program. Before our insurance settlement, we were at a loss for where to go for the best care and how to afford it. We knew Ryan would keep getting better if his therapies continued, but finding the money for them was a big question mark. This dilemma is going on every day for other families, and although we can't help them all, Ryan's Reach wants to help as many as possible.

Ryan once said God was going to use him in a big way, and I believe this is one way God is using him. And here's another: Ryan's little brother, Tyler, worked at High Hopes for a year, helping to care for the students, including Ryan. Just like his dad, Tyler was humble and not afraid to do the dirty work, helping to toilet male students when needed. He says that because he worked at High Hopes, he realized our family isn't the only one that has suffered. Tyler never really had a firm idea of what he wanted to be when he grew up, but after what he's been through with Ryan, he's decided to study health care administration. He wants to make a difference. I know he will.

CHAPTER 14

WE'RE GONNA DANCE

My body is good, but my soul is better.

FROM A RECENT CONVERSATION WITH

RYAN DURING EVENING PRAYERS

CUE MUSIC. The studio lights are beating down on us as we sit across the infamous Larry King interview table. On our first appearance, it wasn't at all certain that Ryan would survive. This time, he sits in his wheelchair, waiting, the big silver microphone on the table in front of him.

Larry's voice, excited, narrates a video of Ryan smiling: "A Christmas miracle! Pat Boone's grandson Ryan speaks for the first time since an accident put him into a coma eighteen months ago." Images flash of Ryan in ICU, covered in bandages, Daddy leaning over him. "Join us for an inspirational update on the emotional story we've followed from the get-go. Ryan Corbin, rendered comatose from a freak fall through the skylight of his condo in June 2001. Now he's out of the hospital and here in our studio.

"Also Ryan's grandfather, Pat Boone, who never lost faith that Ryan would make it." Daddy beams, glowing in a bright yellow sweater, waiting to rejoice with his old friend Larry.

"Ryan's mother, Lindy Boone Michaelis. Ryan's sister, Jessica Corbin. And Ryan's pastor, Rick Warren, on prayer and the power of prayer. The struggle back from the brink of death. Next, on *Larry King Live.*"

After a brief recap of Ryan's accident and the aftermath, Larry looked across the table at Ryan. "We have an amazing result and that is Ryan is here with us tonight looking terrific."

Daddy shared the string of miracles, starting with Ryan's unlikely survival initially, followed by his emergence from what seemed like a hopeless coma, and finally his appearance on the show that night, our fifth visit to Larry King after Ryan's fall.

"We believed all along that he would recover completely and that's what we still believe, and he is doing it," said Daddy.

Jessi explained that Ryan understands everything said to him but can't always respond. He seems to have total recall of everything that happened up until the time of the accident. Ryan watched Larry, followed the conversation, and mouthed the Pledge of Allegiance along with Daddy (his voice was not yet strong). He also said, "Thank you, Larry."

"What is the prognosis, Pat? What do the doctors say now?" Larry asked.

"They can't predict anymore because he's beyond what they predicted," said Daddy.

Larry recalled with amazement how Ryan had looked when Larry had visited him back at CareMeridian. "It's great to see him with us tonight," Larry said, shaking his head in amazement. "He's going to make it."

Larry introduced Rick Warren, pastor of Saddleback

Church and author of *The Purpose Driven Life*. Rick remi-
nisced about Daddy coming to sing at Saddleback when they
first started out in 1980.

"Rick, do you think God played a part in this?" Larry
asked.

"Yes," Rick answered. "These are people of faith, and people
who have a really strong relationship—not a religion—tend to
react to pain differently. You can handle almost anything in life
if you know there is a purpose behind it. That's the real key."

Daddy read from the Bible, a passage that he said had so
much more meaning for him after Ryan's accident:

> Consider it pure joy, my brothers, whenever you
> face trials of many kinds, because you know that
> the testing of your faith develops perseverance.
> Perseverance must finish its work so that you may
> be mature and complete, not lacking anything. . . .
> Blessed is the man who perseveres under trial,
> because when he has stood the test, he will receive
> the crown of life that God has promised to those
> who love him. (James 1:2-4, 12, NIV)

Larry listened closely as Daddy explained that though we
didn't think God *caused* this to happen to Ryan, we believed
he *allowed* it. He could have stopped it but his plan was to
use it for good.

"And he has," Daddy continued, looking straight at Larry,
serious this time. "Partly through you. Largely through you."

"Me, the agnostic," Larry said quietly, eyes locked on
Daddy.

More light conversation. A few questions.

Then Larry asked, "Did you ever think you would lose him?"

I took this one and told Larry no. From the very beginning I thought God was going to do a miracle. Larry seemed shocked when I told him that Ryan goes to church with us, learns the songs and sings along, and helps me take notes, telling me how to spell the words for the fill-in-the-blanks I miss.

As the show came to a close, Larry had a few pointed questions for Pastor Rick. "Why do bad things happen to good people?"

"If I knew everything that God does, I'd be God," said Rick.

The Bible says that life is preparation for eternity, he added. We may have eighty or ninety years on earth but we'll spend trillions of years in eternity. "On earth we practice what we're going to do forever in eternity, and one of those things is grow in character. . . . God specializes in bringing good out of bad. Anyone can bring good out of good."

Rick then verbalized the question people ask whenever there is a tragedy: "Where is God in all this?"

The answer? "He's in his people," said Rick.

Larry nodded and recalled the millions of people around the world who had heard about Ryan and responded.

"Welcome back, Ryan," he said quietly.

✦ ✦ ✦

When Ryan fell through that skylight, it was a catastrophe, an earthquake that shook my life down to its foundation.

When the shaking stopped long enough that I could think rationally again, I had to ask myself, *What do I believe? Does God truly exist?*

I believed in God, so I had two choices: I could get angry and blame him because I believed God caused, or at the very least, allowed his fall. Or I could cooperate with God to find peace in the midst of it and victory over it.

I'm far too practical to go with option number one. This crisis showed me my limitations. I had spent twenty years raising a son who'd become an independent, genuinely good human being who wanted to make a difference in the world. And yet I couldn't keep him from stepping onto a camouflaged skylight that couldn't bear his weight. I couldn't be there to catch him as he fell three stories to concrete. I couldn't be in the operating room to make sure everything was being done to save his life. And once I made it home from Spain to the hospital, there wasn't a thing I could do to wake him up, make him breathe on his own, or get him to move a muscle.

The injuries to my firstborn son would be enough to kill most people, so I was quickly made painfully aware of my limitations. I suppose I could have yelled at God: "How could you let this happen? To Ryan, of all people, one of the dearest people on earth who loved you with abandon. How could you not stop this from happening?"

But that posture would not have done Ryan any good. And as his mother, I wasn't ready to think this was a tragedy with a hopeless ending. To allow bitterness and anger to take over my mind would have meant I was pronouncing Ryan lost to me, crawling in a hole and hiding from the scary world through any means of withdrawal I could find. I understand now why some people choose this option and become addicted to substances that numb the pain. I really do.

My other option was to evaluate where I could find Ryan's best hope of recovery. Certainly we wanted the doctors and nurses to do their utmost to keep him alive, but even they admitted not knowing what the outcome would be. And when they did make predictions, they were often dire.

I had no other choice. I had to look past the earthly answers and rely on heaven's answers. I chose to press in rather than bolt away from all I knew about God. I decided I'd better abandon myself to the idea that God and I were going to go to the next level of our relationship.

I began by looking for evidence of God throughout my life. Where was he? Heaven listened to my mother's tears and faithful prayers when her father died. Heaven heard when I chose to put my faith in Jesus as a young girl afraid of dying.

When I was a confused young mom, heaven heard me play music composed to glorify God when I was trying to find my way back to him. Heaven heard me cry out of my guilt and frustration, even as the songs reminded me that God saw no shame upon me and I could give him all my tomorrows.

Heaven heard a little four-year-old boy call Jesus his Savior and then heard Ryan share his Savior with Mike twenty years later. Heaven prepared Mike to be a strength for me during the biggest event of my life, one that could have taken me down to a pit of despair and serious depression.

Heaven heard the sound of the skylight crashing in and

the sound of Ryan's labored breathing as his body lay crumpled on the concrete. Heaven heard the sirens approaching to take my son to the hospital. Heaven heard the dire prediction of the paramedics to Mama when she arrived at the hospital entrance, and heaven listened as she repeated the words God spoke to her own spirit—"He will *live and not die* and declare the glory of God!"

God and all the hosts of heaven had been with Ryan and our family, not just once we became aware of what happened to Ryan and started to pray, but from the moment we called him the Lord and Savior of our lives.

And once I'd decided to cling to what I knew of God, I looked to him for the strength I needed, minute by minute. Because I was raised in a Christian home and had spent hours in church and Bible study, I knew many verses of Scripture. But I never fully appreciated the value of storing these words in my heart until I had to rely on them to get me through each moment of the day. For the first three months following the accident, Ryan exhibited no purposeful activity at all. Over the next year or two, we lived through one crisis after another. It seemed that whenever Ryan took two steps forward, he'd inevitably take one back. Because he didn't get better very fast, the professionals sometimes lost hope. Progress was slow, and that made the predicted outcome worse. What I saw with my eyes and what I heard from doctors knocked me off my footing.

So I became desperate. The only time I felt in any way secure was when I focused on God's Word. Deuteronomy 8:3 took on new meaning: "People do not live by bread alone; rather, we live by every word that comes from the mouth of the LORD." I could not face the day without soaking in his Word through Bible reading, worship songs, teaching tapes, and prayer. God's Word, written and spoken to my heart, was the only sure foundation I had during those months.

And little by little, I also discovered the influence of my own words. I learned that if the words were fear-based, I should not give them place or power by saying them aloud.

That's what my journal was for. In its pages, I poured out, I vented, I took my burdens to the Lord. I shared some of those entries with you to reveal my darkest hours as a believer, a follower of Jesus, yet also as a human being. God can handle my feelings. In the end, when we get real and honest with God, letting him know we're scared because we don't know how everything's going to turn out, he asks, *But will you trust me anyway?*

As I look back, I'm glad I did. I know that my hope wasn't misplaced and that heaven is at work in Ryan's recovery. I can remember how, time and time again, the Lord delivered Ryan, my family, and me.

While I poured my emotions onto my journal pages, I began editing myself whenever I talked about Ryan's situation. Rather than lamenting how terrible it was, I learned to speak faith-filled words, often and loud. Expecting to see improvement, recovery, and deliverance aligns with the promises of God.

We are made in God's image, and when he speaks, things happen. We are to imitate him, and our words have creative power when we put the force of faith behind them. That is why I spoke life, healing, deliverance, and restoration. I was specific in the words I chose. I remember speaking *appetite* and *voice* over Ryan for two years. I don't do that anymore because now he eats anything and everything and has a loud voice!

Now, over a decade since the accident, Ryan can speak the Word of God himself. One day I came across a verse in the Amplified Bible that jumped out at me. I started calling it Ryan's verse and saying it over him every day:

> This is in keeping with my own eager desire and persistent expectation and hope, that I shall not disgrace myself nor be put to shame in anything; but that with the utmost freedom of speech and unfailing courage, now as always . . . Christ (the Messiah) will be magnified and get glory and praise in this body of mine and be boldly exalted in my person. (Philippians 1:20)

I didn't realize, as I repeated this verse, that Ryan was memorizing it too. The more he heard it, the more he could say the words right along with me. Wow! The fact that my son, who couldn't speak a word for so long, can memorize and speak this powerful verse with understanding is a testimony in and of itself. But beyond this, I believe that by speaking and believing and trusting those words, Ryan is contributing to the fulfillment of these words in his life. Ryan knows who he is, and he still has a committed heart for God. Ryan has a voice, loud and strong, and heaven rejoices to *hear* Ryan speak God's own words back to him.

Through our words, spoken in agreement with the God-inspired words of the apostle Paul, Ryan and I call the

Kingdom of God into our world. I believe Jesus himself modeled praying this way for us. I memorized the Lord's Prayer when I was young, but I have a new understanding of Jesus' words: "Thy kingdom come, Thy will be done in earth, as it *is* in heaven."[27] What is God's will? God's will for us is wholeness. When should we expect his will to be done? On earth as it already *is* in heaven. His Kingdom is *now*.

I still speak faith-filled words over Ryan every night, believing that heaven hears each word I speak over Ryan before he goes to sleep. Currently his short-term memory and cognitive abilities remain limited, he has inconsistent success using the urinal, and he must use a wheelchair to get around. But his biggest challenges today revolve around his moments of angry behavior, which limit his interaction with people and his progress in physical therapy. I suppose that statistically, I could expect Ryan to stay there, stuck, for the rest of his life.

But Ryan has always beaten the statistics. He's shredded them. We've heard negative reports and blown through them more than a few times. So I speak *mobility* until Ryan walks again. I speak *good digestion* until Ryan can avoid seizure reactions to certain foods. I speak *good memory* and *self-control* until he can speak with appropriate politeness and language. And over his legs I speak *strength*, *endurance*, *coordination*, *balance*, and *flexibility* until Ryan is able to stand and walk. Our words matter, and they create the life we will have. I am doing my part to build Ryan up by praying to God these words for him, and I think of myself as a "word layer." (I even used Wordlayer as the handle for my first Twitter account.)

Some days I wonder how long I am to continue speaking such words of life. I've been doing this for eleven years now. Is Ryan going to keep recovering, or is it ever okay to accept things as they are? I have learned to reconcile myself to today's situation and thank God for all I am grateful for at this time. But I can work toward wholeness, and expect improvement and completion. None of us will fully understand the mysteries of healing in this lifetime. Just because healing and wholeness take a while, however, is no reason to decide that God's will is that we accept things *staying* as they are. God's promises don't always happen right away.

Ryan knew that God was planning to use him in a *big* way. He didn't boast, but he shared that conviction with me in confidence. He felt honored and expectant that God had plans to put him in a place that would point large numbers of people toward Christ. Would it be impossible for God to work this part of Ryan's life into the ultimate fulfillment of this vision? Is anything too hard for God?

✦ ✦ ✦

As I wait on the Lord for the rest of what I believe is in store for Ryan, I know I am changing and Ryan is being made ready. Ryan will meet the next milestone, and the next. I continue to speak words of life, strength, restoration, and healing, and so does Ryan.

Recently, I read the story of Jesus and Jairus, a man with a sick daughter who hoped Jesus would come and heal her. On their way to Jairus's home, someone met them to tell them that the little girl had died. The Gospel writer doesn't tell us her father's reaction, but Jesus told the man, "Fear not: believe only" (Luke 8:50, KJV). Then, once he was at the girl's bedside, Jesus raised her from the dead.

If I, like Jairus, reject the fear, I can believe. But if my focus is on how long it's taking, that will lead to fear that healing and wholeness won't ever happen at all. I have to take a stand against anything that develops fear.

Because heaven's timetable is not my own, I must live with the same tension every Christ follower must live with: God's Kingdom has begun to be revealed, but it is not yet fully here. And so I choose to live with the larger reality as my focus. Ultimately I think that's where God wants us to live. He wants us to recognize that our time on earth is temporary, but our existence is eternal.

Not long ago, I discovered that the peacock was an ancient Christian symbol of immortality. Now whenever I see one, I want to praise God, not only for his endless creativity and astonishing use of color, but for the hope I have of spending eternity with Ryan restored to wholeness! Each day, in fact, I relate to Ryan as if he is already restored. This larger perspective enables me to look with the eyes of faith for glimpses of heaven at work here and now.

And what helps me to believe, not fear, is gratitude. I stay, I live, I move, and I breathe, as much as I am able, in thankfulness. Remembering what God has already done builds my faith. Faith then provides an environment ripe for supernatural intervention.

I never felt closer to God than during the eighteen months following the accident. Sometimes I miss the closeness and the intimacy I experienced with God during the time Ryan was in a coma and then began his recovery. Ryan was living on the edge of eternity, so I lived there too. It was the time of greatest growth I've experienced in my fifty-seven years. It was a valley and a mountaintop, all at the same time.

Today Ryan himself often reminds me how close heaven still is to us. One of the best times to get Ryan to focus so we can have a real conversation is at night, when it is quiet and he is settling down for bed. When I'm home I always go into his room and spend time with him. We talk, read the Bible, sing, and pray. One evening we were talking quietly, and I asked Ryan what it means to pray. He said, "Prayer is exercise of the soul."

On another evening, I went into Ryan's room to say good night and tell him that Mike and I were leaving for a class at church that would help us develop our testimony. That way we would be ready to share our faith story with someone when the time came. I asked him, "What is a testimony?"

"It's telling someone about Jesus Christ and getting them into the family."

Well said.

Another night we were taking turns praying quietly, and Ryan prayed, "God, I'm available for whatever you need me for."

✦ ✦ ✦

Last Memorial Day when our family got together, Ryan's stepmom showed us a game on her phone that we could play together with Ryan. It's called Catch Phrase. A word or phrase pops up, and one player has to give clues to the word without actually saying it. I expected Ryan to see the word and automatically read it out loud. But he was easily able to read the word silently, keep it to himself, and give excellent clues for us. He did it again and again. For example, he held his right hand up to his ear with his pinky and thumb extended for one clue. The word was *telephone*. As another clue, he said, "To take something out of thin air and make it." The word was *create*.

And then there was this clue: "A small group of oinkers." Think about it. Got the answer? Yep, the phrase was *three little pigs*. We had a ball celebrating how good he was at giving clues! He has improved so much—I remember when his lack of impulse control wouldn't have allowed him *not* to say the word.

Ryan was in the pool recently with Mike and me. He surprised us by kicking forcefully as he floated on his belly with a Styrofoam noodle underneath. I asked him about it and he said, "Yeah, I had a burst of energy." His therapist got him to repeatedly dive down under the water and retrieve a golf ball on the floor of the pool. It's amazing—he holds his breath as she pushes him underwater, then keeps his eyes open, reaches for the ball, and gets himself back up to the surface.

But don't get me wrong—he can still be contrary at times. He's been exerting his will more and more. His therapist will ask, "Ryan, do you want to go in the pool now?"

"No," he'll say. I think he's disagreeing just on principle. I've also noticed he's getting more discriminating with food, sometimes asking for pizza or spitting out something he doesn't like.

At times he gets stuck in odd behavioral tics, like snapping his fingers, scratching a spot on his face, or rubbing his leg. Sometimes when he does this he'll say, "I'm sorry. I'm sorry." You can tell it's a struggle to live in a body that doesn't do what he wants it to do or does what he doesn't want it to do.

There are some blessings, though. Ryan lives outside of time. As a result, he doesn't think much about the future, so he doesn't mourn the life he lost or the hopes and dreams that were shattered. He remembers he had a girlfriend but doesn't remember the wedding plans. And he never cries or seems sad. Besides occasionally expressing frustration, he's mostly upbeat and joyful, and he still works hard at getting better.

Besides living outside of time, in his mind he isn't aging, either. Ryan thinks he's twenty-four years old. He thinks Tyler is still thirteen, so he's surprised when he realizes, again, that his little brother is now a grown man.

Even I am sometimes surprised when I remember it's been over eleven years since the accident. Life has finally settled into our "new normal." I am back teaching fitness classes and singing with The New Chordettes, a women's quartet reminiscent of the original Chordettes and The Shirelles. I sure have fun onstage with those ladies! Both of these outlets enrich my life and tap into my own gifts. While friends and family always advised me to take time for myself so I'd be better able to cope with the stresses of caregiving, I had to wait until I was ready to be away from Ryan and then reengage in activities that help me relax and recharge.

Ryan's days are pretty full now as well. He spends three mornings a week at High Hopes. In addition, six therapists come to our home to work with Ryan for an hour at a time throughout the week.

Rachael, the wife of one of Ryan's best high school friends and a speech therapist, introduced Ryan to the iPad, e-mail, and Facebook. How wonderful it was to get the flood of messages from friends once they realized Ryan had his own Facebook page! With Rachael's help, Ryan reads the messages and types his responses. Isn't God good?

When he has room in his schedule, Ryan's caregivers place him in the standing frame and stretch him on the mats in our physical therapy room (formerly part of our garage). He can also pedal for up to an hour while sitting in his wheelchair with his feet clipped onto the pedals of an exercise bike or shoot baskets into the hoop on the wall. Every Friday, after a couple of hours of home therapy, Ryan, his caregiver, and I pick a movie to go see. Ryan still loves the movies and it's great to take time to do something just for fun.

A month ago, something new and exciting happened. When we were on *Larry King Live* the last time, Larry asked me, "Will he walk?"

Now, almost ten years later, I have the answer. Larry, this one's for you! Just recently I watched Ryan move his walker on his own from the kitchen down the hall to Mike's office. It was so thrilling to see him lean forward and make that walker go under his own steam. He worked hard, and when he finished, drops of sweat were dripping down his face.

At moments like these, with the eyes of my heart I can see Ryan walking tall and strong, smiling, cracking jokes, and glowing with that Boone-style charisma. Sometimes I think about that night, long ago, around my parents' big round maple dining table. "I Hope You Dance" plays again in my head, and I treasure the memory of us dancing, all of us celebrating Ryan and Jessi moving on, leaving the nest and flying into adulthood. God has promised me that Ryan and I will dance again. I know it. I feel it. He's not there yet, but I'm still seeing progress. We all are.

As Ryan walked himself across the threshold into Mike's office, I asked him how he felt.

He smiled that big Ryan smile and said, his voice warm and deep, "I feel like I accomplished something."

You did, Son. You did. You are going to walk and then . . . we're gonna dance!

Afterword

BY DEBBY BOONE

IF YOU ARE ANYTHING LIKE ME, you had to wipe some tears from your eyes as you read Lindy's closing words. The progress we have seen in Ryan is nothing short of miraculous, but it is the transformation I have seen in my sister that moves and challenges me most.

Personally speaking, I am increasingly uncomfortable with the human need to explain inexplicable tragedy, but I am encouraged, literally given courage, by Lindy's story of acceptance, gratitude, and pursuit of wholeness for herself and for Ryan. Lindy has grabbed hold of the kind of faith that can take her through anything, a trust that defies certainty, peace that passes understanding.

Several years ago, on a five-day spiritual retreat, I was asked to take a psalm and put it into my own words out of my own personal experience. It was a powerful exercise that required me to examine my heart, drop pretenses, tell the truth, and accept my powerlessness. From that place I was able to turn things over to God. I love the psalms, and I identify with the heart's cry in so many of them . . . fear, failure, confusion, anger and resentment, joy, gratitude, trust. This is the music of our lives, and there is beauty in even the most sorrowful song.

After finishing *Heaven Hears*, I felt as if I had just read Lindy's version of Psalm 23, written in her own words and out of her own experiences. Lindy has shared from her heart the truth of her journey of learning to trust God no matter what, as he transforms her into her most beautiful, whole self. In her introduction Lindy said that this is a story about "overcoming despair, persisting through suffering, and surviving against all odds."

Are you sinking into despair? Do you need strength to persist even though it looks like all the odds are against you? I encourage you to write your own psalm. There is nothing you can't say, nothing you need to keep to yourself . . . God can take it.

You just need to let him.

Just after Lindy finished writing her book, she rediscovered a journal entry I had sent her one month after Ryan had his accident. I would like to share a little of it with you because it is coming from a perspective Lindy did not have access to, someone watching her go through the unimaginable. I was experiencing a vulnerability I had never felt before Ryan's fall. I had become acutely aware of what a friend of mine once called "the paper thinness of life." During that time, I stayed at my own home to sleep and did only what absolutely had to be done. The rest of the time I wanted to be in the waiting room at UCLA. I wrote:

Amidst the pain and the suffering, there has been
something so beautiful, so powerful that it has transcended

everything else. I don't know if I can describe adequately what it was exactly, but I know it had to do with family and friends coming together in love, with faith and hope that runs deeper than our deepest fears. Ironically, it's as if we all were awakened out of our own comas, out of our numbness to what life is really all about. No more just getting through the day with our "to do" lists never being completed and spilling over to the next day's agenda. Suddenly we were awake and aware, dropping anything and everything that had seemed so important, so necessary—to gather in a room together, mostly on our knees. Connection with each other and with God was all that mattered. That is still all that matters.

In that room we encountered the presence of God as we shared Scriptures, sang old hymns, prayed, and hugged. I saw something in Lindy that was so charismatic—there is no other word for it. I have always suspected, or I guess I should say hoped, that if ever I had to face real tragedy, I would receive from God comfort and strength beyond anything I've ever had before because I would need it more than ever. When I am with Lindy, I know now that this is not false hope. I love being with her, and I'm sure it's because I see Jesus in her eyes. I feel his presence when I'm around her. And I can barely tear myself away.

Almost all of my life I have read and sung the words of Psalm 27, and there have been inspired moments when they actually felt like the true desire of my heart. But in the middle of this experience, it is truly as if these words have become flesh in Lindy:

One thing have I asked of the Lord, that will I seek, inquire for, and [insistently] require: that I may dwell in the house of the Lord [in His presence] all the days of my life, to behold and gaze upon the beauty [the sweet attractiveness and the delightful loveliness] of the Lord and to meditate, consider, and inquire in His temple.

For in the day of trouble He will hide me in His shelter; in the secret place of His tent will He hide me; He will set me high upon a rock.

And now shall my head be lifted up above my enemies round about me; in His tent I will offer sacrifices and shouting of joy; I will sing, yes, I will sing praises to the Lord.

Hear, O Lord, when I cry aloud; have mercy and be gracious to me and answer me!

You have said, Seek My face [inquire for and require My presence as your vital need]. My heart says to You, Your face [Your presence], Lord, will I seek, inquire for, and require [of necessity and on the authority of Your Word]. (verses 4-8, AMP)

When I am with Lindy, who has sought the face of the Lord because his presence has been her vital need, I behold the beauty, the sweet attractiveness, and the delightful loveliness of the Lord. He has hidden her in his shelter, in the secret place of his tent. Daily I see her lifted up above her fears, offering sacrifices and shouts of joy. And she sings. And we all sing with her our praises to the Lord.

When Ryan is awake and strong—and he will be—my

prayer is that I won't, that we won't, slip back into our own comas, losing our close connection with one another and the Lord. But we are human beings and tend not to require his presence or one another's presence when we are not vitally in need of it. Through this experience, we have all been changed "in the secret place of His tent," and in our day of trouble we know exactly where to run. Each time we do, we will come a little closer to learning that his shelter is not only the place we run to, but a place where we can dwell.

God invites you into his shelter, and the psalms are a great way to get there. The more time you spend there, the more it feels like home.

Acknowledgments

I would love to express my appreciation to so many people who have taken part in the creation of *Heaven Hears*. I don't know where to begin so I'll begin with the people God used to lead me toward a book deal.

Thank you, Sue Nelson, for hearing the Holy Spirit, who prompted you to e-mail me; for sharing your excitement that I had written a book; and for presenting me with a name and contact so I could pursue a publisher. Without that e-mail, this book would not have been widely available.

Then I must thank Don Otis, Sue's friend, who encouraged me to seek a traditional route to publish this story. I had no contacts and no clue for how to do that. Thank you, Don, for encouraging me to utilize a coauthor and get the book in a form that would be ready for a larger audience. Thank you for introducing me to Susy Flory and for your continued input and encouragement along the way.

Of course I want to thank Susy Flory for the hours and hours of reading about my family. You must know more about my life now than I can recall living. You have taken my loaves-and-fishes of a story and created a much more filling and completely balanced meal, adding more background and family perspective to the manuscript I originally wrote. I am so glad to have been able to share this journey with you and to have your gifts contribute to the telling of this story.

I also must thank Chip MacGregor for being our literary agent and for guiding me through the business end of getting a book to the readers. I am a mom, a singer, and a fitness instructor. The world of book publishing is a foreign land to me, so thank you for being a wonderful guide.

Thank you to the people I have met with Tyndale House

Publishers: Jon Farrar, Kim Miller, Kara Leonino, Cheryl Kerwin, and Maggie Rowe. It is an honor to have such a group of established professionals work with me and take such an interest in *Heaven Hears*. I have been very heard and respected during this process. I am humbled by the number of people who have poured their time and expertise into something that I thought I'd written just as an exercise to process the last decade and possibly share with a few people I meet along the way. Thank you for recognizing the bigger picture and supporting me as my own vision has grown.

Now I will try to express my depth of gratitude to some of the leading players in this story.

To every doctor, nurse, aide, and therapist who has been involved with Ryan's care since he fell and lay in a coma, my everlasting thanks.

To Mark Desmond, I thank you for the hours and hours of hands-on work you do with Ryan and all the students at High Hopes; for building this place where families like mine can be allowed to hope for better recovery.

To James, Joseph, Chris, and Erwin (who took over for Joseph when he returned to the Philippines)—what can I say? You have been the angels I prayed for. What you have given of yourselves beyond the call of duty as caregivers is something I could never adequately compensate in this lifetime. I do expect the Lord to bless you abundantly, and your treasures in heaven will know no bounds.

To Larry King, I am forever grateful that you gave my family a forum to express our love of God, our faith in a crisis, and our joy as Ryan came on with us for that fifth television program. Whether you know it or not, God used you in a very impactful way, and I will never forget what it meant to have people all over the world pray for my son to recover. I am in your debt.

How can I thank my most amazing family? I am blessed beyond words. I thank you, Doug, for being on the front lines and for taking the bullets and protecting me from some of the harshest words from the doctors. I am so glad you and Vic are two of my best friends.

It's absolutely impossible to find words to express what my parents have meant to me but here is my best effort. For raising me to know God, to love him and lean on him, and to know his promises, I give you my undying thanks. Daddy, you have lived your life in such a way that you are an inspiration to many and you are loved around the world. I know Ryan was brought to the world's stage because of your presence on it, and I thank you for using your platform to request prayer for Ryan's recovery. Mama, you are my hero for the hours and hours you spent with Ryan at the hospital and other facilities so I could take time away. For loving him so much that you understood every pain and every joy along the way that I experienced. For loving me enough to stop your life and live through the terrible uncertainty of coma and traumatic brain injury. For never accepting a bad report but always remembering the Word of God that takes precedence over it all.

Thank you, Cherry, Debby, and Laury. At different times each of you showed up, lifted my spirits, and shared your wisdom and love with me in critical moments. But my special deep appreciation goes to Debby, the other middle child, the sister I shared a room with. You showed up for me in so many ways to bring me into the presence of the Lord, to make me feel less alone, to even make me laugh when laughing seemed practically impossible. I will always remember and I will be there for you, too.

Lastly, I couldn't make it without Mike, Jessi, and Tyler. You and Ryan are the completion of who I am. I am so proud of my three children and so grateful that we have made it through and have such a strong love. We took a beating, that's for sure. Mike, my love, there is nobody like you. I love you dearly and I am incredibly blessed to be sharing my life with you.

Heavenly Father, I thank you for your Word, which is life. Thank you for Ryan's verse as we have applied it to his situation: "Do not gloat over me, my enemies! For though I fall, I will rise again. Though I sit in darkness, the LORD will be my light" (Micah 7:8).

Lindy Boone Michaelis

✦ ✦ ✦

When I was a girl, I read an unforgettable book about a young athlete who dove into shallow water in Chesapeake Bay and broke her neck. She became a quadriplegic and struggled with depression. She later came to terms with her injury and learned to paint with a brush in her mouth. The book was *Joni* by Joni Eareckson Tada and that story stays with me still. One thing she said shocked me—Joni was thankful for her accident because she experienced God's presence and power in a way she never had before. God gave her the grace she needed to persist through unspeakable tragedy. "God doesn't just give us grace," she says. "He gives us Jesus, the Lord of grace." That grace and that raw, close-to-the-bone experience of God is what I see in Lindy's story, along with the accompanying deep wisdom. Lindy, thank you for letting me be a part of sharing your story. And Ryan, thank you for teaching me to never give up.

My thanks to Lindy's family, who opened up their hearts and, often through tears, told me their stories: Jessica, Tyler, Mike, Doug, and Debby. Mr. and Mrs. Boone, thank you for making me feel welcome and serving me a wonderful lunch around that big, round maple table. I expected to feel nervous meeting you but I didn't; you felt like family.

I'm grateful to Steve Sawalich for sharing, for the first time in print, your memory of that day. Thanks to Mark Desmond, director of High Hopes, for showing me around and introducing me to students and instructors. And to Chris, one of Ryan's caretakers, for answering my pesky questions with a smile.

Kathleen Brandon, you were a huge help with deciphering Ryan's complicated medical records. And to the readers' group for *Heaven Hears*—Kristy, Kelly, Ellen, Claire, Melanie, Cathi, Vickie, and Tracy—we couldn't have done it without you. Thank you so much for reading the manuscript when it was still pretty rough.

Don, your mountaineering exploits kept me entertained

during the work on this book. Thank you for introducing me to Lindy's story. And Chip, my agent and friend, I really enjoy working with you. Thanks for taking a chance on me those years ago, even though we still haven't worked out our differences on Twain vs. Fitzgerald. And the Tyndale folks have been wonderful. Jon, Kim, and Kara, I enjoyed our rainy day lunch and I know Lindy and Ryan's story is in very good hands.

Susy Flory

Where Are They Now?

Pat Boone is a singer, actor, TV host, producer, songwriter, author, motivational speaker, TV pitchman, radio personality, record company head, TV station owner, sports team owner, family man, humanitarian, and a man unafraid to air his views. He still goes to his office every day, makes media and live appearances, plays tennis and golf, and maintains a tan. See http://www.patboone.com.

Shirley Boone is a loving wife, proud mother, and doting grandmother. Shirley and Pat have been married fifty-nine years and have lived in the same Beverly Hills house for over fifty years. Shirley is a prayer warrior and very active in her faith community at The Church on the Way in Van Nuys, California.

Cherry (Boone) O'Neill, the oldest of the four Boone sisters, currently resides in Sammamish, Washington, with her husband, Dan O'Neill, founder of the humanitarian relief and development organization Mercy Corps (www.mercycorps.org). Together they have raised five children: Brittany, Brendan, Casey, Kevyn, and Kylie. Cherry's book *Starving for Attention*, about her personal struggle with anorexia and bulimia, made the *New York Times* Best Sellers List in the early eighties. Cherry recently started her own life coaching business, Active Transformation (www.active-transformation.com), and facilitates a monthly parent networking group. She serves in youth ministry and sings in the choir at her church.

Lindy (Boone) Michaelis lives in Southern California with her husband of twenty-seven years, attorney Mike Michaelis. She has three adult children: Ryan, Jessi, and Tyler. Lindy has worked in the fitness industry as a personal trainer and group fitness instructor. She also tours with a singing group called The New Chordettes, performing songs with tight harmonies from the forties, fifties, and sixties. Lindy is a founding board member and active fund-raiser for Ryan's Reach, the Ryan Corbin Foundation for Brain Injury.

Debby (Boone) Ferrer earned instant fame when her first single, "You Light Up My Life," was an overnight hit in 1977. The tune claimed the number one spot on the Billboard charts for ten straight weeks and sold in excess of four million copies. Debby received the Grammy Award for Best New Artist of the Year, and has since won two additional Grammy Awards and seven Grammy nominations. In addition to her recording career, Debby has acted in starring roles on Broadway and continues to perform before live audiences. She has been married to Gabriel Ferrer for thirty-three years, and they have four grown children. See http://debbyboone.net.

Laury (Boone) Browning teaches eighth grade English in Fort Collins, Colorado, where she currently resides with her husband, Dr. Aaron Koepp, an established chiropractor in the area. Laury and Aaron enjoy beach vacations, skiing, and riding motorcycles in their scenic hometown. She is happiest spending time with her husband and adult children: son, Michael (and his wife, Ashley, and their children, Jeremiah and Rebekah), and twin daughters, Sara and Rachael.

Doug Corbin lives in Dove Canyon, California, with his wife, Victoria, and daughter, Alyssa. He was formerly the assistant vice chancellor for estate and gift planning at Pepperdine University and is currently president of Paragon Charitable Services Group, Inc., where he provides fund development consulting services for charitable organizations throughout Southern California. Doug is also a cofounder and president of Ryan's Reach, the Ryan Corbin Foundation for Brain Injury.

Ryan Corbin lives at home with Lindy and Mike Michaelis, where he works full-time toward complete recovery. In his spare time he enjoys spending time with his family, going to the movies every Friday, and watching his Lakers play basketball.

Jessica Corbin is an integrated fitness expert, TV host and producer, and an entrepreneur. Passionate about helping people become more healthy and fit, she released her first mobile fitness technology called Vitness Rx in the fall of 2012. She currently lives in Marina Del Rey, California. See http://vitnessrx.com.

Tyler Michaelis lives in Newport Beach, California, and works at a substance abuse treatment center. He's attending

Cal State–Long Beach with a major in health care administration. Tyler is close to getting his certification as a drug and
alcohol counselor and would like to work in a health care–
related field. He hopes to help many sick people recover.

Mike Michaelis falls deeper in love with his beautiful wife,
Lindy, each and every day. He is semiretired, still representing a limited number of new-vehicle-dealer clients. He vol-
unteers regularly with the legal assistance program offered
through his church. Mike remains physically active through
his love of golf and skiing, on both snow and water.

Steven Sawalich, Ryan's close friend and roommate who was
with him when he fell, is executive director of the Starkey
Hearing Foundation. He is a philanthropist whose career
merges a devotion to international humanitarian aid and
capturing key elements of the human experience on film.
He studied acting at the prestigious Royal Academy of
Dramatic Art in London and performed at the Edinburgh
Fringe Festival in Scotland in the critically acclaimed plays
A Streetcar Named Desire and *So Mr. Brecht, What Did You
Think of America?* Sawalich, who was mentored by the late
Sydney Pollack and Paul Newman, later formed Articulus
Entertainment, which released the award-winning film *Music
Within* to critical acclaim.

Notes

1. *Larry King Live*, August 17, 2001
2. Romans 5:3-4
3. Paul Davis, *Pat Boone: The Authorized Biography* (London: Harper Collins, 2001), 39.
4. Shirley Boone, *One Woman's Liberation* (Savage, MN: Lighthouse Christian Publishing, 2009), 82.
5. Davis, *Pat Boone*, 69.
6. Pat and Shirley Boone, *The Honeymoon Is Over* (Savage, MN: Lighthouse Christian Publishing, 2009), 47.
7. I won't tell their stories in detail because they've written about it themselves in Daddy's book *A New Song* (Creation House, 1972) and Mama's story, *One Woman's Liberation*. But I was a witness to the power of God to restore a marriage and to replace fear with faith.
8. Mama's book, *One Woman's Liberation*, came out in 1972.
9. Second Chapter of Acts, "Which Way the Wind Blows," on the album *With Footnotes*, recorded 1974.
10. Keith Green, "When I Hear the Praises Start," on the album *For Him Who Has Ears to Hear*, released May 20, 1977. © EMI Music Publishing.
11. The screenplay's title was inspired by John 3:16 (NIV): "For God so loved the world that he gave his one and only Son, that whoever believes in him shall not perish but have eternal life."
12. Richard Preston, *The Wild Trees* (New York: Random House, 2007), 15.
13. Ibid., 98.
14. John 11:21-24, author's paraphrase.
15. Benny Hinn, *The Miracle of Healing* (Nashville: Thomas Nelson, 1998), 17 (italics in the original).
16. Note on Psalm 40:1-3 in the *Life Application Study Bible* (Carol Stream, IL: Tyndale House Publishers, 1988).
17. Romans 5:4
18. He was referring to Exodus 14, the account of how God miraculously delivered Moses and the Israelites when the pursuing Egyptians had cornered them at the Red Sea.
19. "NINDS Coma Information Page," National Institute of Neurological Disorders and Stroke, National Institutes of Health, last updated September 18, 2012, http://www.ninds.nih.gov/disorders/coma/coma.htm.

20. From the New Century Version.
21. From the Amplified Bible.
22. Mark Faul, Likang Xu, Marlena M. Wald, and Victor G. Coronado, *Traumatic Brain Injury in the United States: Emergency Department Visits, Hospitalizations and Deaths 2002–2006* (Atlanta: Centers for Disease Control and Prevention, National Center for Injury Prevention and Control; 2010), 7.
23. Ibid.
24. "Traumatic Brain Injury: The Journey Home," The Center of Excellence for Medical Multimedia, Defense Health Board, http://www.traumatic braininjuryatoz.org/Resource-Center/Frequently-Asked-Questions.aspx.
25. "Living with Brain Injury," Brain Injury Association of American, http://www.biausa.org/living-with-brain-injury.htm.
26. Cited in "Injury Prevention and Control: Traumatic Brain Injury," Centers for Disease Control and Prevention, last updated September 21, 2012, http://www.cdc.gov/traumaticbraininjury/severe.html.
27. Matthew 6:10, KJV, emphasis added.

About the Authors

Lindy Boone Michaelis was born into an entertainment environment as the second daughter of singer/entertainer Pat Boone and grew up in Beverly Hills, California. She and her family toured all over the United States and around the world. The Boone Girls recorded several Christian albums, including the Grammy Award–nominated *First Class*. Lindy is wife to Mike and mother to Ryan, Jessica, and Tyler. Since Ryan's fall through the skylight of his apartment building, Lindy has learned a lot about traumatic brain injury (TBI) and come to a new understanding of the faithfulness of God during our deepest needs. The Boone family has established a foundation in Ryan's name, called Ryan's Reach, to help survivors of brain injury and their families.

Susy Flory is a *New York Times* bestselling author with degrees from UCLA in English and psychology. She taught high school English and journalism, then began writing full time in 2004, writing for publications such as *Focus on the Family*, *Guideposts Books*, and *Today's Christian Woman*. Susy's first book, *Fear Not Da Vinci*, was cowritten with Gini Monroe and published in 2006. Other books include *So Long, Status Quo: What I Learned from Women Who Changed the World* (2009); *Dog Tales: Inspirational Stories of Humor, Adventure, and Devotion* (2011); and the runaway bestseller *Thunder*

Dog: The True Story of a Blind Man, His Guide Dog, and the Triumph of Trust at Ground Zero (2011), cowritten with Michael Hingson. Susy is a member of the American Society of Journalists and Authors (ASJA) and a CLASS certified speaker. She lives in the San Francisco Bay area with her husband, Robert, and their two children.

RYAN'S
REACH

Ryan's Reach is an organization that seeks to aid brain-injured individuals and their families by providing financial resources and promotional support to High Hopes Neurological Recovery Group, Inc., a public charitable organization based in Orange County, California. We are committed to expanding the programs, services, and outreach of High Hopes Neurological Recovery Group to more effectively address the financial, emotional, physical, and spiritual needs of traumatic brain injury victims and their families.

Ryan's Reach envisions moving beyond the status of a supporting organization to becoming a charity, thereby allowing the foundation to establish a home (or homes) serving brain-injured adults and their families. The vision is to provide a safe and comfortable environment where families can bring their brain-injured loved ones for a few hours or days of respite care, being assured they will be properly cared for. Such a home would allow families an opportunity to get some well deserved rest and relaxation from the daily routine of personally caring for their loved ones.

For further information on therapies and treatments for people with traumatic brain injuries and to see how you can get involved, please visit RYANSREACH.COM.